The Uttermost

Marie Belloc Lowndes

Alpha Editions

This edition published in 2024

ISBN : 9789362093646

Design and Setting By
Alpha Editions
www.alphaedis.com
Email - info@alphaedis.com

Contents

I.

Laurence Vanderlyn, unpaid attaché at the American Embassy in Paris, strode down the long grey platform marked No. 5, of the Gare de Lyon. It was seven o'clock, the hour at which Paris is dining or is about to dine, and the huge station was almost deserted.

The train de luxe had gone more than an hour ago, the Riviera rapide would not start till ten, but one of those trains bound for the South, curiously named demi-rapides, was timed to leave in twenty minutes.

Foreigners, especially Englishmen and Americans, avoid these trains, and this was why Laurence Vanderlyn had chosen it as the starting point of what was to be a great adventure, an adventure which must for ever be concealed, obliterated as much as may be from his own memory—do not men babble in delirium?—once life had again become the rather grey thing he had found it to be.

In the domain of the emotions it is the unexpected which generally happens, and now it was not only the unexpected but the incredible which had happened to this American diplomatist. He and Margaret Pargeter, the Englishwoman whom he had loved with an absorbing, unsatisfied passion, and an ever-increasing concentration and selfless devotion, for seven years, were about to do that which each had sworn, together and separately, should never come to pass,—that is, they were about to snatch from Fate a few days of such free happiness and communion as during their long years of intimacy they had never enjoyed. In order to secure these fleeting moments of joy, she, the woman in the case, was about to run the greatest risk which can in these days be incurred by civilised woman.

Margaret Pargeter was not free as Vanderlyn was free; she was a wife,—not a happy wife, but one on whose reputation no shadow had ever rested,—and further, she was the mother of a child, a son, whom she loved with an anxious tenderness.... It was these two facts which made what she was going to do a matter of such moment not only to herself, but to the man to whom she was now about to commit her honour.

Striding up and down the platform to which he had bought early access by one of those large fees for which the travelling American of a certain type is famed, Vanderlyn, with his long lean figure, and stern pre-occupied face, did not suggest, to the French eyes idly watching him, a lover,—still less the happy third in one of those conjugal comedies which play so much greater a part in French literature and in French drama than they do in French life. He had thrust far back into his heart the leaping knowledge of what was about to befall him, and he was bending the whole strength of his mind to avert any possible danger of ignoble catastrophe to the woman whom he was awaiting, and whose sudden surrender was becoming more, instead of less, amazing as the long minutes dragged by.

Vanderlyn's mind went back to the moment, four short days ago, when this journey had been suddenly arranged. Mrs. Pargeter had just come back from England, where she had gone to pay some family visits and to see her little son, who was at a preparatory school; and the American diplomatist, as was so often his wont, had come to escort her to one of those picture club shows in which Parisian society delights.

Then, after a quarter of an hour spent by them at the exhibition, the two friends had slipped away, and had done a thing which was perhaps imprudent. But each longed, with an unspoken eager craving, to be alone with the other; the beauty of Paris in springtime tempted them, and it was the woman who had proposed to the man that they should spend a quiet hour walking through one of those quarters of old Paris unknown to the travelling foreigner.

Eagerly Vanderlyn had assented, and so they had driven quickly down the Rue de Rivoli, right into the heart of that commercial quarter which was the Paris of Madame de Sévigné, of the bitter witty dwarf, Scarron, of Ninon de l'Enclos, and, more lately, of Victor Hugo. There, dismissing their cab, they had turned into that still, stately square, once the old Place Royale, now the Place des Vosges, of which each arcaded house garners memories of passionate romance.

Walking slowly up and down the solitary garden there, the two had discussed the coming August, and Margaret Pargeter had admitted, with a rather weary sigh, that she was as yet quite ignorant whether her husband intended to yacht, to shoot, or to travel,—whether he meant to take her with him, or to leave her at some seaside place with the boy.

As she spoke, in the low melodious voice which still had the power to thrill the man by her side as it had had in the earlier days of their acquaintance, Mrs. Pargeter said no word that all the world might not have heard, yet, underlying all she said, his questions and her answers, was the mute interrogation—which of the alternatives discussed held out the best chance, to Vanderlyn and herself, of being together?

At last, quite suddenly, Mrs. Pargeter, turning and looking up into her companion's face, had said something which Laurence Vanderlyn had felt to be strangely disconcerting; for a brief moment she lifted the veil which she had herself so deliberately and for so long thrown over their ambiguous relation—"Ah! Laurence," she exclaimed with a sigh, "the way of the transgressor is hard!"

Then, speaking so quietly that for a moment he did not fully understand the amazing nature of the proposal she was making to him, she had deliberately offered to go away with him—for a week. The way in which this had come about had been strangely simple; looking back, Vanderlyn could scarcely believe that his memory was playing him true....

From the uncertain future they had come back to the immediate present, and Mrs. Pargeter said something of having promised her only intimate friend, a Frenchwoman much older than herself, a certain Madame de Léra, to go and spend a few days in a villa near Paris—"If you do that," he said, "then I think I may as well go down to Orange and see the house I've just bought there."

She had turned on him with a certain excitement in her manner. "You've bought it? That strange, beautiful place near Orange where you used to stay when you were studying in Paris? Oh, Laurence, I'd no idea that you really meant to buy it!"

A little surprised at the keenness of her interest, he had answered quietly, "Yes, when the owner was going through Paris last week, I found he wanted the money, so—so the house is mine, though none of the legal formalities have yet been complied with. I'm told that the old woman who was caretaker there can make me comfortable enough for the few days I can be away." He added in a different, a lower tone, "Ah! Peggy, if only it were possible for us to go there together—how you would delight in the place!"

"Would you like me to come with you? I will if you like, Laurence." She had asked the question very simply—but Vanderlyn, looking at her quickly, had seen that her hand was trembling, her eyes brimming with tears. Then she had spoken gently, deliberately—seeming to plead with herself, rather than with him, for a few days of such dual loneliness for which all lovers long and which during their long years of intimacy they had never once, even innocently, enjoyed. And he had grasped with exultant gratitude—what man would have done otherwise?—at what she herself came and offered him.

Walking up and down the solitary platform, Vanderlyn lived over again each instant of that strange momentous conversation uttered four days ago in the stately sunlit square which forms the heart of old Paris. How the merry ghost of Marion Delorme, peeping out of one of the long narrow casements of the corner house which was once hers, must have smiled to hear this virtuous Englishwoman cast virtue to the light Parisian winds!

Vanderlyn also recalled, with almost the same surprise and discomfort as he had experienced at the time itself, the way in which Margaret Pargeter, so refined and so delicately bred, had discussed all the material details connected with their coming adventure—details from which the American diplomatist himself had shrunk, and which he would have done almost anything to spare her.

"There is one person, and one alone," she had said with some decision, "who must know. I must tell Adèle de Léra—she must have my address, for I cannot remain without news of my boy a whole week. As for Tom"—she had flushed, and then gone on steadily—"Tom will believe that I am going to stay with Adèle at Marly-le-Roi, and my letters will be sent to her house. Besides," she had added, "Tom himself is going away, to England, for a fortnight."

To the man then walking by her side, and even now, as he was remembering it all, the discussion was inexpressibly odious. "But do you think," he had ventured to ask, "that Madame de Léra will consent? Remember, Peggy, she is Catholic, and what is more, a pious Catholic."

"Of course she won't like it—of course she won't approve! But I'm sure—in fact, Laurence, I *know*—that she will consent to forward my letters. She understands that it would make no difference—that I should think of some other plan for getting them. Should she refuse at the last moment—but—but she will not refuse—" and her face—the fair, delicately-moulded little face Vanderlyn loved—had become flooded with colour.

For the first time since he had known her, he had realised that there was a side to her character of which he was ignorant, and yet?—and yet Laurence Vanderlyn knew Margaret Pargeter too well, his love of her implied too intimate a knowledge, for him not to perceive that something lay behind her secession from an ideal of conduct to which she had clung so unswervingly and for such long years.

During the four days which had elapsed between then and now,—days of agitation, of excitement, and of suspense,—he had more than once asked himself whether it were possible that certain things which all the world had long known concerning Tom Pargeter had only just become revealed to Tom Pargeter's wife. He hoped, he trusted, this was not so; he had no desire to owe her surrender to any ignoble longing for reprisal.

The world, especially that corner of Vanity Fair which takes a frankly materialistic view of life and of life's responsibilities, is shrewder than we generally credit, and the diplomatist's intimacy with the Pargeter household had aroused but small comment in the strange polyglot society in which lived, by choice, Tom Pargeter, the cosmopolitan millionaire who was far more of a personage in Paris and in the French sporting world than he could ever have hoped to be in England.

To all appearance Laurence Vanderlyn was as intimate with the husband as with the wife, for he had tastes in common with them both, his interest in sport and in horseflesh being a strong link with Tom Pargeter, while his love of art, and his dilettante literary tastes, bound him to Peggy. Also, and perhaps above all, he was an American—and Europeans cherish strange and sometimes fond illusions as to your American's lack of capacity for ordinary human emotion.

He alone knew that his tie with Mrs. Pargeter grew, if not more passionate, then more absorbing and intimate as time went on, and he was sometimes, even now, at considerable pains to put the busybodies of their circle off the scent.

But indeed it would have required a very sharp, a very keen, human hound to find the scent of what had been so singular and so innocent a tie. Each had schooled the other to accept all that she would admit was possible. True, Vanderlyn saw Margaret Pargeter almost every day, but more often than not in the presence of acquaintances. She never came to his rooms, and she had never seemed tempted to do any of the imprudent things which many a woman, secure of her own virtue, will sometimes do as if to prove the temper of her honour's blade.

So it was that Mrs. Pargeter had never fallen into the ranks of those women who become the occasion for even good-natured gossip. The very way in which they had, till to-night, conducted what she, the woman, was pleased to call their friendship, made this which was now happening seem, even now, to the man who was actually waiting for her to join him, as unsubstantial, as likely to vanish, mirage-wise, as a dream.

And yet Vanderlyn passionately loved this woman whom most men would have thought too cold to love, and who had known how to repress and tutor, not only her own, but also his emotions. He loved her, too, so foolishly and fondly that he had fashioned the whole of his life so that it should be in harmony with hers, making sacrifices of which he had told her nothing in order that he might surround her—an ill-mated, neglected wife—with a wordless atmosphere of devotion which had become to her as vital, as necessary, as is that of domestic peace and happiness to the average woman. But for Laurence Vanderlyn and his "friendship," Mrs. Pargeter's existence would have been lacking in all human savour, and that from ironic circumstance rather than from any fault of her own.

Vanderlyn had spent the day in a fever of emotion and suspense, and he had arrived at the Gare de Lyon a good hour before the time the train for Orange was due to leave.

At first he had wandered about the great railway-station aimlessly, avoiding the platform whence he knew he and his companion were to start. Then, with relief, he had hailed the moment for securing coming privacy in the unreserved railway carriage; this had not been quite an easy matter to compass, for he desired to avoid above all any appearance of secrecy.

But he need not have felt any anxiety, for whereas in an English railway-station his large "tip" to the guard, carrying with it significant promise of final largesse, would have spelt but one thing, and that thing love, the French railway employé accepted without question the information that the lady the foreign gentleman was expecting was his sister. Such a statement to the English mind would have suggested the hero of an innocent elopement, but as regards family relations the French are curiously Eastern, and then it may be said again that the American's stern, pre-occupied face and cold manner were not those which to a Parisian could suggest a happy lover.

As he walked up and down with long, even strides, his arms laden with papers and novels, it would have been difficult for anyone seeing him there to suppose that Vanderlyn was starting on anything but a solitary journey. Indeed, for the moment he felt horribly alone. He began to experience the need of human companionship. She had said she would be there at seven; it was now a quarter-past the hour. In ten minutes the train would be gone——

Then came to him a thought which made him unconsciously clench his hands. Was it not possible, nay, even likely, that Margaret Pargeter, like many another woman before her, had found her courage fail her at the last moment—that Heaven, stooping to her feeble virtue, had come to save her in spite of herself?

Vanderlyn's steps unconsciously quickened. They bore him on and on, to the extreme end of the platform. He stood there a moment staring out into the red-starred darkness: how could he have ever thought that Margaret Pargeter—his timid, scrupulous little Peggy—would embark on so high and dangerous an adventure?

There had been a moment, during that springtime of passion which returns no more, when Vanderlyn had for a wild instant hoped that he would be able to take her away from the life in which he had felt her to be playing the terrible rôle of an innocent and yet degraded victim.

Even to an old-fashioned American the word divorce does not carry with it the odious significance it bears to the most careless Englishwoman. He had envisaged a short scandal, and then his and Peggy's marriage. But he had been compelled, almost at once, to recognise that with her any such solution was impossible.

As to another alternative? True, there are women—he and Margaret Pargeter had known many such—who regard what they call love as a legitimate distraction; to them the ignoble, often sordid, shifts involved in the pursuit of a secret intrigue are as the salt of life; but this solution of their tragic problem would have been—or so Vanderlyn would have sworn till four days ago—impossible to the woman he loved, and this had added one more stone to the pedestal on which she had been placed by him from the day they had first met.

And yet? Yet so inconsequent and so illogical is our poor human nature, that she, the virtuous woman, had completely lacked the courage to break with the man who loved her, even in those, the early friable days of their passion. Nay more, whatever Peggy might believe, Vanderlyn was well aware that the good, knowing all, would have called them wicked, even if the wicked, equally well-informed, would have sneered at them as absurdly good.

Vanderlyn wheeled abruptly round. He looked at the huge station clock, and began walking quickly back, down the now peopled platform to the ticket barrier. As he did so his eyes and mind, trained to note all that was happening round him, together with an unconscious longing to escape from the one absorbing thought, made him focus those of his fellow-travellers who stood about him. They consisted for the most part of provincial men of business, and of young officers in uniform, each and all eager to prolong to the uttermost their golden moments in Paris; more than one was engaged in taking an affectionate, deeply sentimental farewell from a feminine companion who bore about her those significant signs—the terribly pathetic, battered air of wear and tear—which set apart, in our sane workaday world, the human plaything.

The sight of these leave-takings made the American's face flush darkly; it was hateful to him to think that Mrs. Pargeter must suffer, even for a few moments, the proximity of such women—of such men. He felt a violent shrinking from the thought that any one of these gay, careless young Frenchmen might conceivably know Peggy—if only by sight—as the charming, "elegant" wife of Tom Pargeter, the well-known sportsman who had done France the signal honour of establishing his racing stable at Chantilly instead of at Newmarket! The thought that such an encounter was within the bounds of possibility made Vanderlyn for a moment almost hope that the woman for whom he was waiting would not come after all.

He cursed himself for a fool. Why had he not thought of driving her out to one of the smaller stations on the line whence they could have started, if not unseen, then unobserved?

But soon the slowly-growing suspicion that she, after all, was perhaps not coming to-night, brought with it an agonising pang. Very suddenly there occurred to him the horrible possibility of material accident. Mrs. Pargeter was not used even to innocent adventure; she lived the guarded, sheltered existence which belongs of right to those women whose material good fortune all their less fortunate sisters envy. The dangers of the Paris streets rose up before Vanderlyn's excited imagination, hideous, formidable....

Then, quite suddenly, Margaret Pargeter herself stood before him, smiling a little tremulously.

She was wearing a grey, rather austere tailor-made gown; it gave a girlish turn to her slender figure, and on her fair hair was poised the little boat-shaped hat and long silvery gauze veil which have become in a sense the uniform of a well-dressed Parisienne on her travels.

As he looked at her, standing there by his side, Vanderlyn realised how instinctively tender, how passionately protective, was his love for her; and again there came over him the doubt, the questioning, as to why she was doing this....

"Messieurs, mesdames, en voiture, s'il vous plaît! En voiture, s'il vous plaît!"

He put his hand on her shoulder—her head was very little higher than his heart—and guided her to the railway carriage which had been kept for them.

II.

And now Laurence Vanderlyn and Margaret Pargeter were speeding through the night, completely and physically alone as they had never been during the years of their long acquaintanceship; and, as he sat there, with the woman he had loved so long and so faithfully wholly in his power, there came over Vanderlyn a sense of fierce triumph and conquest.

The train had not started to time. There had come a sound of eager talking on the platform, and Vanderlyn, filled with a vague apprehension, had leaned out of the window and with some difficulty ascertained the cause of the delay. The guard in charge of the train, the man, that is, whom he had feed so well in order to secure privacy, had strained his hand in lifting a weight, and another employé had had to take his place.

But at last the few moments of waiting—to Vanderlyn they had seemed an hour—had come to an end. At last the train began to move, that slow and yet relentless movement which is one of the few things in our modern world which spell finality. To the man and the woman it was the starting of the train which indicated to them both that the die was indeed cast.

Vanderlyn looked at his companion. She was gazing up at him with a strange expression of gladness, of relief, on her face. The long years of restraint and measured coldness seemed to have vanished, receded into nothingness.

She held out her ringless hand and clasped his, and a moment later they were sitting hand in hand, like two children, side by side. With a rather awkward movement he slipped on her finger a thin gold ring—his dead mother's wedding-ring,—but still she said nothing. Her head was turned away, and she was staring out of the window, as if fascinated by the flying lights. He knew rather than saw that her eyes were shining, her cheeks pink with excitement; then she took off her hat, and he told himself that her fair hair gleaming against the grey-brown furnishings of the railway carriage looked like a golden aureole.

Suddenly Laurence Vanderlyn pressed the hand he was holding to his lips, dropped it, and then stood up. He pulled the blue silk shade over the electric light globe which hung in the centre of the carriage; glanced through one of the two tiny glazed apertures giving a view of the next compartment; then he sat down by her, and in the half darkness gathered her into his arms.

"Dear," he said, in a voice that sounded strange and muffled even to himself, "do you remember the passage at Bonnington?"

As he held her, she had been looking up into his face, but now, hearing his question, she flushed deeply, and her head fell forward on his breast. Their minds, their hearts, were travelling back to the moment, to the trifling episode, which had revealed to each the other's love.

It had happened ten years ago, at a time when Tom Pargeter, desiring to play the rôle of country gentleman, had taken for awhile a certain historic country house. There, he and his young wife had brought together a great Christmas house-party composed of the odd, ill-assorted social elements which gather at the call of the wealthy host who has exchanged old friends for new acquaintances. Peggy's own people, old-fashioned country gentry, were regarded by Pargeter as hopelessly dowdy and "out of it," so none of them had been invited. With Laurence Vanderlyn alone had the young mistress of the house had any link of mutual interests or sympathies; but of flirtation, as that protean word was understood by those about them, there had been none.

Then, on Christmas Eve, had come the playing of childish games, though no children were present, for the two-year-old child of the host and hostess was safe in bed. It was in the chances of one of these games that Laurence Vanderlyn had for a moment caught Margaret Pargeter in his arms——

He had released her almost at once, but not before they had exchanged the long probing look which had told to each their own as well as the other's secret. Till that moment they had been strangers—from that moment they were lovers, but lovers allowing themselves none of love's license, and very soon Vanderlyn had taught himself to be content with all that Peggy's conscience allowed her to think possible.

She had never known—how could she have known?—what his acquiescence had cost him. Now and again, during the long years, they had been compelled to discuss the abnormal relation which Peggy called their friendship; together they had trembled at the fragile basis on which what most human beings would have considered their meagre happiness was founded.

More than once she had touched him to the heart by asserting that she felt sure that the inscrutable Providence in which she had retained an almost childish faith, could never be so cruel as to deprive her of the only source of happiness, apart from her little son, which had come her way; and so, although their intimacy had become closer, the links which bound them not only remained platonic, but, as is the way with such links, tended to become more platonic as the time went on. ———

Even now, as he sat there with the woman he loved wholly in his power, lying in his arms with her face pressed to his breast, Vanderlyn's mind was in a maze of doubt as to what was to be their relationship during the coming days. Even now he was not sure as to what Peggy had meant when she had seemed to plead, more with herself than with him, for a short space of such happiness as during their long intimacy they had never enjoyed.

All his acquaintances, including his official chief, would have told you that Laurence Vanderlyn was an accomplished man of the world, and an acute student of human nature, but now, to-night, he owned himself at fault. Only one thing was quite clear; he told himself that the thought of again taking up the thread of what had been so unnatural an existence was hateful—impossible.

Perhaps the woman felt the man's obscure moment of recoil; she gently withdrew herself from his arms. "I'm tired," she said, rather plaintively, "the train sways so, Laurence. I wonder if I could lie down——"

He heaped up the cushions, spread out the large rug, which he had purchased that day, and which formed their only luggage, for everything else, by her wish, had been sent on the day before.

Very tenderly he wrapped the folds of the rug round her. Then he knelt by her side; and at once she put out her arms, and pulled his head down close to hers; a moment later her soft lips were laid against his cheek. He remembered, with a retrospective pang, the ache at his heart with which the sight of her caresses to her child had always filled him.

"Peggy," he whispered, "tell me, my beloved, why are you being so good to me—now?"

She made no direct answer to the question. Instead, she moved away a little, and raised herself on her elbow; her blue eyes, filled with a strange solemnity, rested on his moved face.

"Listen," she said, "I want to tell you something, Laurence. I want you to know that I understand how—how angelic you have been to me all these years. Ever since we first knew one another, you have given me everything—everything in exchange for nothing."

And as he shook his head, she continued, "Yes, for nothing! For a long time I tried to persuade myself that this was not so—I tried to believe that you were as contented as I had taught myself to be. I first realised what a hindrance"—she hesitated for a moment, and then said the two words—"our friendship—must have proved to you four years ago,—when you might have gone to St. Petersburg."

As Vanderlyn allowed an exclamation of surprise to escape him, she went on, "Yes, Laurence, you have never known that I knew of that chance—of that offer. Adèle de Léra heard of it, and told me; she begged me then, oh! so earnestly, to give you up—to let you go."

"It was no business of hers," he muttered, "I never thought for a moment of accepting——"

"——But you would have done so if you had never known me, if we had not been friends?" She looked up at him, hoping, longing, for a quick word of denial.

But Vanderlyn said no such word. Instead, he fell manlike into the trap she had perhaps unwittingly laid for him.

"If I had never known you?" he repeated, "why, Peggy—dearest—my whole life would have been different if I had never known you! Do you really think that I should have been here in Paris, doing what I am now doing—or rather doing nothing—if we had never met?"

The honest, unmeditated answer made her wince, but she went on, as if she had not heard it—

"As you know, I did not take Adèle's advice, but I have never forgotten, Laurence, some of the things she said."

A look which crossed his face caused her to redden, and add hastily, "She's not given to speaking of you—of us; indeed she's not! She never again alluded to the matter; but the other day when I was persuading her,—she required a good deal of persuasion, Laurence—to consent to my plan, I reminded her of all she had said four years ago."

"And what was it that she did say four years ago?" asked Vanderlyn with a touch of angry curiosity; "as Madame de Léra is a Frenchwoman, and a pious Catholic, I presume she tried to make you believe that our friendship was wrong, and could only lead to one thing——" he stopped abruptly.

"No," said Peggy, quietly, "she did not think then that our friendship would lead to—to this; she thought in some ways better of me than I deserve. But she did tell me that I was taking a great responsibility on myself, and that if anything happened—for instance, if I died——" Vanderlyn again made a restless, almost a contemptuous movement—"I should have been the cause of your wasting the best years of your life; I should have broken and spoilt your career, and all—all for nothing."

"Nothing?" exclaimed Vanderlyn passionately. "Ah! Peggy, do not say that. You know, you must know, that our love—I will not call it friendship," he went on resolutely, "for this one week let no such false word be uttered between us—you must know, I say, that our love has been everything to me! Till I met you, my life was empty, miserable; since I met you it has been filled, satisfied, and that even if I have received what Madame de Léra dares to call—nothing!"

He spoke with a fervour, a conviction, which to the woman over whom he was now leaning brought exquisite solace. At last he was speaking as she had longed to hear him speak.

"You don't know," she whispered brokenly, "how happy you make me by saying this to-night, Laurence. I have sometimes wondered lately if you cared for me as much as you used to care?"

Vanderlyn's dark face contracted with pain; he was no Don Juan, learned in the byways of a woman's heart. Then, almost roughly, he caught her to him, and she, looking up, saw a strange glowing look come over his face—a look which was, even to her, an all-sufficing answer, for it told of the baffled longing, of the abnegation, and, even now, of the restraint and selflessness, of the man who loved her.

"Did you really think that, Peggy?" was all he said; then, more slowly, as the arms about her relaxed their hold, "Why, my dear, you've always been—you are—my life."

A sudden sob, a cry of joy broke from her. She sat up, and with a quick passionate movement flung herself on his breast; slowly she raised her face to his: "I love you," she whispered, "Laurence, I love you!"

His lips trembled for a moment on her closed eyelids, then sought and found her soft, quivering mouth. But even then Vanderlyn's love was reverent, restrained in its expression, yet none the less, perhaps the more, a binding sacrament.

At last, "Why did you subject us," he said, huskily, "to such an ordeal? What has made you give way—now? How can you dream of going back, after a week, to our old life?" But even as he asked the searching questions, he laid her back gently on her improvised couch.

Woman-like she did not give him a direct response, then, quite suddenly, she yielded him the key to the mystery.

"Because, Laurence, the last time I was in England, something happened which altered my outlook on life."

She uttered the words with strange solemnity, but Vanderlyn's ears were holden; true, he heard her answer to his question, but the word conveyed little or nothing to him.

He was still riding the whirlwind of his own poignant emotion; he was telling himself, with voiceless and yet most binding oaths, that never, never should the woman whose heart had just beaten against his heart, whose lips had just trembled beneath his lips, go back to act the part of even the nominal wife to Tom Pargeter. He would consent to any condition imposed by her, as long as they could be together; surely even she would understand, if not now, then later, that there are certain moments which can never be obliterated or treated as if they have not been....

It was with difficulty—with a feeling that he was falling from high heaven to earth—that he forced himself to listen to her next words.

"As you know, I stayed, when in England, with Sophy Pargeter———"

Again she looked up at him, as if hesitating what she should say.

"Sophy Pargeter?" he repeated the name mechanically, but with a sudden wincing.

Vanderlyn had always disliked, with a rather absurd, unreasoning dislike, Peggy's plain-featured, rough-tongued sister-in-law. To him Sophy Pargeter had ever been a grotesque example of the deep—they almost appear racial—differences which may, and so often do, exist between different members of a family whose material prosperity is due to successful commerce.

The vast inherited wealth which had made of Tom Pargeter a selfish, pleasure-loving, unmoral human being, had transformed his sister Sophy into a woman oppressed by the belief that it was her duty to spend the greater part of her considerable income in what she believed to be good works. She regarded with grim disapproval her brother's way of life, and she condemned even his innocent pleasures; she had, however, always been fond of Peggy. Laurence Vanderlyn, himself the outcome and product of an old Puritan New England and Dutch stock, was well aware of the horror and amazement with which Miss Pargeter would regard Peggy's present action.

"Well, Laurence, the day that I arrived there, I mean at Sophy's house, I felt very ill. I suppose the journey had tired me, for I fainted———" Again she hesitated, as if not knowing how to frame her next sentence.

"Sophy was horribly frightened. She would send for her doctor, and though he said there was nothing much the matter with me, he insisted that I ought to see another man—a specialist."

Peggy looked up with an anxious expression in her blue eyes—but again Vanderlyn's ears and eyes were holden. He habitually felt for the medical profession the unreasoning dislike, almost the contempt, your perfectly healthy human being, living in an ailing world, often—in fact almost always—does feel for those who play the rôle of the old augurs in our modern life. Mrs. Pargeter had never been a strong woman; she was often ill, often in the doctor's hands. So it was that Vanderlyn did not realise the deep import of her next words———

"Sophy went with me to London—she was really very kind about it all, and you would have liked her better, Laurence, if you had seen her that day. The specialist did all the usual things, then he told me to go on much as I had been doing, and to avoid any sudden shock or excitement—in fact he said almost exactly what that dear old French doctor said to me a year ago——"

She waited a moment: "Then, Laurence, the next day, when Sophy thought I had got over the journey to London," Peggy smiled at him a little whimsical smile, "she told me that she thought I ought to know—it was her duty to tell me—that I had heart disease, and that, though I should probably live a long time, it was possible I might die at any moment——"

A sudden wrath filled the dark, sensitive face of the man bending over her.

"What nonsense!" he exclaimed with angry decision. "What will the doctors say next, I wonder! I wish to God you would make up your mind, Peggy, once and for all, never to see a doctor again! I beg of you, if only for my sake, to promise me that you will not go again to any doctor till I give you permission to do so. You don't know what I went through five years ago when one of those charlatans declared that he would not answer for the consequences if you didn't winter South, and—and Tom would not let you go!"

He paused, and then added more gently, "And yet nothing happened—you were none the worse for spending that winter in cold Leicestershire!"

"Yes, that's true," she answered submissively, "I will make you the promise you ask, Laurence. I daresay I have been foolish in going so often to doctors; I don't know that they have ever done me much good."

His eyes, having now become quite accustomed to the dim light, suddenly seemed to see in her face a slight change; a look of fatigue and depression had crept over her mouth. He told himself with a pang that after all she was a delicate, fragile human being—or was it the blue shade which threw a strange pallor on the face he was scrutinising with such deep, wistful tenderness?

He bent over her and tucked the rug round her feet.

"Turn round and try to go to sleep," he whispered. "It's a long, long journey by this train. I'll wake you in good time before we get to Dorgival."

She turned, as he told her, obediently, and then, acting on a sudden impulse, she pulled him down once more to her, and kissed him as a child might have done. "Good night," he said, "good night, my love—'enchanting, noble little Peggy!'"

A smile lit up her face radiantly. It was a long, long time since Vanderlyn had last uttered the charming lines first quoted by him very early in their acquaintance, when he had seen her among her own people, one of a band of joyous English boys and girls celebrating a family festival—the golden wedding of her grandparents. Peggy had been delicately, deliciously kind to the shy, proud American youth, whom an introduction from valued friends had suddenly made free of an English family clan.

That had been a year before her marriage to Tom Pargeter, the inheritor of a patent dye process which had made him master of one of those fantastic fortunes which impress the imagination of even the unimaginative. That the young millionaire should deign to throw the matrimonial handkerchief at their little Peggy had seemed to her family a piece of magic good fortune. She could bring him good old blood, and certain great social connections, in exchange for limitless wealth; it had been regarded as an ideal marriage.

More than four years went by before Vanderlyn again saw Peggy, and then he had found her changed—transformed from a merry, light-hearted girl into a pensive, reserved woman. During the interval he had often thought of her as one thinks of a delightful playfellow, but he only came to love her after their second meeting—when he had seen, at first with honest dismay, and then with shame-faced gladness, how utterly ill-mated she and Tom Pargeter were the one to the other.

Vanderlyn made his way over to the other side of the railway carriage; there he sat down, and, crossing his arms on his breast, after a very few moments he fell into a deep, dreamless sleep.

III.

Vanderlyn woke with a start. He looked round, bewildered for a moment. Then his brain cleared, and he felt vexed with himself, a little ashamed of having slept. It seemed to him that he had been asleep hours. How odious it would have been if at the first stopping place of the demi-rapide some stranger had entered the railway carriage! Instead of sleeping, he ought to have remained watching over that still figure which lay so quietly resting on the other side of the carriage.

He stood up. How tired he felt, how strangely depressed and uneasy! But that, after all, was natural, for his last four nights had been wakeful, his last four days full of anxiety and suspense.

He turned and looked out of the window, wondering where they were, how far they had gone; the train was travelling very quickly, he could see white tree-trunks rushing past him in the moonlight.

Then Vanderlyn took out his watch. Surely it must be later than nine o'clock? He moved from the window and held the dial close under the blue silk shade of the lamp. Why, it was only three minutes to nine! Then they hadn't yet passed Dorgival; in fact they wouldn't be there for another twenty minutes, for this train took two hours to do what the quick expresses accomplished in an hour and a quarter.

It was good to know that he had only slept for quite a little while. The desire for sleep had now left him completely, and he began to feel excited, restless, and intensely, glowingly alive....

The curious depression and unease which had possessed him a few moments ago lifted from his soul; the future was once more full of infinite possibilities.

His darling little Peggy! What strange beings women were! With what self-contempt, with what scorpions would he have lashed himself, had he been the one to evolve this plan of this furtive flight, to be followed at the end of a week by a return to the life to which he now looked back with shame as well as distaste! And yet she, the woman he loved, had evolved it, and thought out every detail of the scheme—before telling him of what was in her mind...

As to the future? Vanderlyn threw back his head; nay, nay, there could be no going back to what had been. Even Peggy would see that. She had herself broken down the barrier erected with such care; and soon, very soon she would—she must—see that such breaches can never be repaired or treated as if they had not been made. What had happened, what was happening, to-night, was, in very truth the beginning, for them both, of a new life.

So Laurence Vanderlyn swore to himself, taking many silent vows of chivalrous devotion to the woman who, for love of him, had broken, not only with life-long traditions of honour, but also with a conscience he had known to be so delicately scrupulous.

From where he was standing in the middle of the swaying carriage, something in the way in which his sleeping companion's head was lying suddenly aroused Vanderlyn's quick, keen attention. Putting out a hand to steady himself against the back of the compartment, he bent down—indifferent to the risk of rousing the still figure.

Then, with a rapid movement, he straightened himself; his face had gone grey—expressionless. He pushed back the blue shade off the globe of light, careless of the bright rays which suddenly illumined every corner of the railway carriage....

With an instinctive gesture, Vanderlyn covered his eyes and shut out the blinding light. He pressed his fingers on his eyeballs; every fibre of his body, every quivering nerve was in revolt: for he realised, even then, that there was no room for hope, for doubt,—he knew that what he had looked upon in the dim light was death.

With an awful pang he now understood why Peggy had made him that strange pathetic offer. How blind he had been! The English doctor, the man on whom he had poured such careless scorn, had been right,—terribly right.

At last he uncovered his eyes, and forced himself to gaze upon what lay before him——

Margaret Pargeter had died in her sleep. She was lying exactly as Vanderlyn had left her, still folded closely in the rug he had placed so tenderly about her. But a terrible change had come over the delicate features—the sightless eyes were wide open, the lips had fallen apart; his glance, travelling down, saw that her left hand, the hand where gleamed his mother's wedding ring, was slightly clenched.

Again Vanderlyn passed his hand over his eyes. He stared about him with a touch of helpless bewilderment, but he could do nothing, even if there had been anything to do; it was she who had insisted that they should be unencumbered by any luggage.

He crouched down, and, with an involuntary inward shrinking, took up the chilly, heavy hand and tried to warm it against his cheek; then he shivered, his teeth chattered, with a groan of which the sound echoed strangely in his ears he hid his face in the folds of her grey cloth gown——For a few moments the extent of his calamity blotted out everything.

And then, as Vanderlyn lay there, there suddenly opened before him a way of escape from his intolerable agony and sense of loss, and he welcomed it with eager relief. He raised his head, and began to think intently. How inexplicable that he had not thought of this—the only way—at once! It was so simple and so easy; he saw himself flinging wide open the narrow carriage door, and then, with that still figure clasped in his arms, stepping out into the rushing darkness....

His mind was now working with incredible quickness and clearness. How good it was to know that here, in France, there need be—there would be—no public scandal! In England or America the supposed suicide of two such people as were Margaret Pargeter and himself could not hope to be concealed; not so in France.

Here, as Vanderlyn knew well, there was every chance that such a love tragedy as the one of which he and Mrs. Pargeter would be supposed to have been hero and heroine, would remain hidden—hidden, that is, from everyone except those closely connected with her and with himself. His own chief, the American Ambassador, would be informed of what had happened, but he was a wise old man, there was no fear of indiscretion in that quarter; but—yes, he, Vanderlyn, must face that fact—Tom Pargeter would know the truth.

Vanderlyn's hidden abhorrence of *the other man*,—of the man whose friend he had perforce compelled himself to be for so long, rose in a great flood.

Tom Pargeter? The selfish, mean-souled, dull-witted human being, whose huge fortune, coupled with the masculine virtues of physical courage and straightness in matters of sport, made him not only popular but in a small way a personage! Pargeter, no doubt, would suffer, especially in his self-esteem; on the other hand, he, the husband, would feel that so had his own conduct, his coarse infidelity, his careless neglect of his wife, been fully condoned.

With a choking feeling of sharp pain, Vanderlyn suddenly remembered that what Tom Pargeter knew now, poor Peggy's son would some day have to know. For awhile, no doubt, the boy would be kept in merciful ignorance of the tragedy, but then, when the lad was growing into manhood, some blundering fool, or more likely some well-intentioned woman, probably his aunt, Sophy Pargeter, would feel it her duty to smirch for him his mother's memory....

Nay, that could not, that must never, be! Vanderlyn's head fell forward on his breast; there came back, wrapping him as in a shroud, the awful feeling of desolation, of life-long loss,—for he now knew, with inexorable knowledge, what the future held for him.

It must be his fate to live, not die; he must live in order to safeguard the honour of Margaret Pargeter, the beloved woman who had trusted him wholly, not only in this, which was to have been their supreme adventure, but during the whole of their long, almost wordless love. It was for her sake that, she dead, he must go on living; for her sake he must make what now, at this moment, seemed to be a sacrifice almost beyond his power, for reason told him that he must leave her, and as soon as possible, lying there dead—alone.

With tender, absent fingers he smoothed out the woollen folds to which his face had been pressed; he slipped from her finger the thin gold ring, and placed it once more where he had always worn it from the day of his mother's death till an hour ago.

Then he stood up, and turned deliberately away.

There came the loud wailing whistle which told that the train was nearing a station. He leaned out of the window; the lights of a town were flashing past, and he grimly told himself that there was no time to lose.

Vanderlyn again bent down; the instinctive repugnance of the living for the dead suddenly left him. His darling little Peggy! How could he bear to leave her there—alone? If he and she had been what they ought to have been—husband and wife—even then, he felt that never would he have left her to the neglect, to the forgetfulness to which other men leave their beloved dead. There rose before him the memory of one of the most moving of the world's great pictures, Goya's painting of mad Queen Joan bearing about with her the unburied body of Philip.

He turned that which had been Margaret Pargeter so that her face would be completely hidden from anyone opening the door and looking into the carriage.

Yet, even as he was doing this, Vanderlyn kept a sharp watch and ward over his own nerves. His had now become the mental attitude of a man who desires to save the living woman whom he loves from some great physical danger. Blessing his own foresight in providing the large rug which he had folded about her so tenderly an hour ago, he pulled up a fold of it till it covered, and completely concealed, her head. Should a traveller now enter the carriage he would see nothing but a woman apparently plunged in deep slumber.

Again Vanderlyn glanced, with far more scrutinising eyes than he had done when first entering the train, through the two glazed apertures which commanded a view of the next carriage; it was, as he knew well, empty.

He turned once more the silk shade over the lamp, jammed his hat down over his eyes, set his lips together, and, averting his eyes from what he was leaving, opened the railway carriage door....

The train was slowing down; a few hundred yards ahead lay the station. Vanderlyn stepped to one side of the footboard, and waited till the door through which he had just passed swung to; then he turned the handle, securing it firmly.

With soft, swift steps, he walked past the window of the now darkened carriage and slipped into the next empty, brightly-lighted compartment. There came over him a strong temptation to look through the little apertures giving into the darkened carriage he had just left, but it was a temptation which he resisted. Instead, he leant out of the window, as does a traveller who is nearing his destination.

Soon there floated up to him the shouting of "Dorgival! Cinq minutes d'arrêt!" and when the train at last stopped, there arose the joyous chatter which attends every arrival in a French station.

Vanderlyn waited for a few moments; then he stepped down from the carriage, and began walking quietly down the platform. With intense relief he remembered that the guard of the train whom he had feed so well, and who must have noticed him with Peggy, had been left behind in Paris.

Having passed the end compartment and guard's van he stood for awhile staring down at the permanent way, counting the rails which gleamed in the half darkness. He measured with his eyes the distance which separated the platform on which he was standing from that whence the next train back to Paris must start.

There was very little risk either of accident or detection, but it was his duty to minimise whatever risk there was. He dropped down gently onto the permanent way, and stood for a moment in the deep shadow cast by the rear of the train he had just left; then, cautiously advancing, he looked both up and down the line, and made his way to the other side.

The platform on which he now found himself was deserted, for the whole life of the station was still centred round the train which had just arrived; but as he started across the rails Vanderlyn became possessed with a feeling of acute, almost intolerable, suspense. He longed with a feverish longing to see the demi-rapide glide out into the darkness. He told himself he had been a fool to suppose that anyone could enter the darkened carriage where the dead woman lay without at once discovering the truth,—and he began asking himself what he would do were the awful discovery made, and were the fact that he had been her travelling companion suddenly revealed or suspected.

But Laurence Vanderlyn was not subjected to so dread an ordeal; at last there floated to where he was standing the welcome cry of "En voiture! En voiture, s'il vous plaît!" The dark serpentine mass on which the lonely man's eyes were fixed shivered as though it were a sentient being waking to life, and slowly the train began to move.

Vanderlyn started walking up the platform, and for awhile he kept in step with the slowly gliding carriages; then they swept by more quickly, a swift procession of gleaming lights....

As at last the red disc melted into the night, he gave a muffled groan of anguish, for mingling with his sense of intense relief, came that of eternal, irreparable loss.

Ironic fortune was kind to Vanderlyn that night; his return ticket from far-away Orange, though only issued in Paris some two hours before, was allowed to pass unchallenged; and a couple of francs bestowed on a communicative employé drew the welcome news that a southern express bound for Paris was about to stop at Dorgival.

IV.

It was only eleven o'clock when Vanderlyn found himself once more in the Gare de Lyon. He walked quickly out of the great station which was henceforth to hold for him such intimately tender and poignant memories; and then, instead of taking a cab, he made his way on foot down to the lonely Seine-side quays.

There, leaning over and staring down into the swift black waters of the river, he planned out his drab immediate future.

In one sense the way was clear before him,—he must of course go on exactly as before; show himself, that is, in his usual haunts; take the moderate part he had hitherto taken in what he felt to be the dreary round of so-called pleasures with which Paris was now seething. That must be his task—his easy and yet intolerable task—during the next week or ten days, until the disappearance of Margaret Pargeter became first suspected, and then discovered.

But before that was likely to happen many long days would certainly go by, for,—as is so often the case when a man and woman have become, in secret, everything to one another, Laurence Vanderlyn and Mrs. Pargeter had gradually detached themselves from all those whom they had once called their friends, and even Peggy had had no intimate who would miss a daily, or even a weekly, letter.

Indeed, it was just possible, so Vanderlyn, resting his arms on the stone parapet, now told himself, that the first part of his ordeal might last as long as a fortnight, that is, till Tom Pargeter came back from England.

There was of course yet another possibility; it was conceivable that everything would not fall out as they, or rather Peggy, had imagined. Pargeter, for instance, might return sooner; and, if he did so, he would certainly require his wife's immediate presence in Paris, for the millionaire was one of those men who hate to be alone even in their spare moments. Also more than his wife's company, Pargeter valued her presence as part of what the French so excellently style the *décor* of his life; she was his thing, for which he had paid a good price; some of his friends, the sycophants with which he loved to be surrounded, would have said that he had paid for her very dearly.

It was very unlikely, however, that Tom Pargeter would return to Paris before he was expected to do so. For many years past he had spent the first fortnight of each May at Newmarket; and, as is the curious custom of his kind, he seldom varied the order of his rather monotonous pleasures.

But stay—Vanderlyn suddenly remembered Madame de Léra, that is the one human being who had been in Peggy's confidence. She was a real and terrible point of danger—or rather she might at any moment become so. It was with her, at the de Léra villa in the little village of Marly-le-Roi, that Mrs. Pargeter was, even now, supposed to be staying. This being so, he, Vanderlyn, must make it his business to see Madame de Léra at the first possible moment. Together they would have to concoct some kind of possible story—he shuddered with repugnance at the thought.

Long before Peggy's confidences in the train, the American diplomatist had been well aware that Adèle de Léra disapproved of his close friendship with Mrs. Pargeter; and she had never lent herself to any of those innocent complicities with which even good women are often so ready to help those of their friends who are most foolish—whom perhaps they know to be more tempted—than themselves.

The one thing of paramount importance, so Vanderlyn suddenly reminded himself, was that no one—not even Madame de Léra—should ever know that he and Margaret Pargeter had left Paris that night, together. How could this fact be best concealed, and concealed for ever?

To the unspoken question came swift answer. It flashed on the man lingering on the solitary river-side quay, that even now, to-night, it was not too late for him to establish the most effectual of alibis. By taking a fiacre and bribing the man to drive quickly he could be back in his rooms in the Rue de Rivoli, dressed, and at his club, before midnight. Fool that he was to have wasted even a quarter of an hour!

Vanderlyn struck sharply across the dimly-lighted thoroughfare; he started walking down one of the narrow streets which connect the river quays with commercial Paris. A few moments later, having picked up a cab, he was driving rapidly westward, down the broad, still seething Boulevard du Temple, and, as he suddenly became aware with a sharp pang at his heart, past the entrance to the quiet mediæval square, where, only four short days ago, he and Peggy walking side by side, had held the conversation which was to prove pregnant of so much short-lived joy, and of such long-lived pain.

Like so many modern Americans, to whom every material manifestation of wealth has become distasteful, Laurence Vanderlyn had chosen to pitch his Paris tent on the top floor of one of those eighteenth-century houses which, if lacking such conveniences as electric light and lifts, can command in their place the stately charm and spaciousness of which the modern Parisian architect seems to have lost the secret. His *appartement* consisted of a few large, airy, low-pitched rooms, of which the stone balconies overlooked the Tuileries gardens, while from a corner window of his sitting-room Vanderlyn could obtain what was in very truth a bird's-eye view of the vast Place de la Concorde.

Very soon after his arrival in Paris the diplomatist had the good fortune to come across a couple of French servants, a husband and wife, who exactly suited his simple and yet fastidious requirements. They were honest, thrifty, clean, and their only fault—that of chattering to one another like magpies—was to Vanderlyn an agreeable proof that they led a life quite independent of his own. Never had he been more glad to know that this was so than to-night, for they greeted his return home with the easy indifference, and real pleasure, very unlike the surface respect and ill-concealed resentment with which a master's unexpected appearance would have been received by a couple of more cosmopolitan servitors.

With nerves strung up to their highest tension, forcing himself only to think of the present, Vanderlyn put on his evening clothes. It was still wanting some minutes to midnight when he left the Rue de Rivoli for the Boulevard de la Madeleine. A few moments later he was at the door of the club where he was sure of finding, even at this time of night, plenty of friends and acquaintances who would be able to testify, in the very unlikely event of its being desirable that they should do so, to the fact that he had been there that evening.

L'Union is the most interesting, as it is in a certain sense the most exclusive, of Paris clubs. Founded in memory of the hospitality shown by the English gentry to the French émigrées, during the Revolution, this, the most old-fashioned of Paris clubs, impales the Royal arms of France, that is, the old fleur-de-lys, with those of England.

At all times L'Union has been in a special sense a resort of diplomatists, and Vanderlyn spent there a great deal of his spare time. The American was popular among his French fellow-members, to whom his excellent French and his unobtrusive good breeding made him an agreeable companion. There could have been no greater proof of how he was regarded there than the fact that, thanks to his efforts, Tom Pargeter had been elected to the club. True, the millionaire-sportsman did not often darken the threshold of the stately old club-house, but he was none the less exceedingly proud of his membership of L'Union, for it gave him an added standing in the cosmopolitan world in which he had early elected to spend his life. Perhaps it was fortunate that he had so little use for a club where gambling games are not allowed to be played—where, indeed, as the younger members are apt to complain, dominoes take the place of baccarat!

The tall Irish footman whose special duty it was to wait on the foreign members, came forward as Vanderlyn walked into the hall. "Mr. Pargeter has been asking for you, sir; he's in the card-room."

Vanderlyn felt a curious sensation sweep over him. That which he had thought so improbable as to be scarcely worth consideration had come to pass. Pargeter had not gone to England that night. He was here, in Paris, at L'Union, asking for him. In a few moments they would be face to face.

As Vanderlyn walked up the broad staircase, he asked himself, with a feeling of agonising uncertainty, whether it was in any way possible that Peggy's husband had found out, even suspected, anything of their plan. But no! Reason told him that such a thing was quite inconceivable. No compromising word had been written by the one to the other, and every detail had been planned and carried out in such a way as to make discovery or betrayal impossible.

But to-night reason had very little to say to Laurence Vanderlyn, and his strongly drawn face set in hard lines as he sauntered through now fast thinning rooms, for the habitué of L'Union generally seeks his quiet home across the Seine about twelve.

As he returned the various greetings which came to him from right and left,—for a French club has about it none of the repressive etiquette which governs similar institutions in England and America,—the diplomatist felt as doubtless feels any imaginative man who for the first time goes under fire; what he experienced was not so much dread as a wonder how he was likely to bear himself during this now imminent meeting with Peggy's husband.

Suddenly Vanderlyn caught sight of Pargeter, and that some moments before he himself was seen by him. The millionaire was standing watching a game of whist, and he looked as he generally looked when at L'Union, that is, bored and ill at ease, but otherwise much as usual.

Tom Pargeter was a short man, and though he was over forty, his fair hair, fat face, and neat, small features gave him an almost boyish look of youth. He had one most unusual physical peculiarity, which caused him to be remembered by strangers: this peculiarity consisted in the fact that one of his eyes was green and the other blue. His manners were those of a boy, of a boorish lad, rather than of a man; his vocabulary was oddly limited, and yet he seldom used the correct word, for he delighted in verbal aliases.

Seeing Pargeter there before him, Laurence Vanderlyn, for the first time in his life, learned what so many men and women learn very early in their lives,—what it is to be afraid of a person, who, however despicable, is, or may become, your tyrant.

Hitherto his relations with Peggy's husband, though nothing to be proud of, had brought with them nothing of conscious shame. Nay more, Laurence Vanderlyn, in that long past of which now nothing remained, had tried to see what was best in a character which, if fashioned meanly, was not wholly bad.

But now, to-night, he felt that he despised, hated, and, what was to him, far worse, feared the human being towards whom he was advancing with apparently eager steps.

Suddenly the eyes of the two men met, but Pargeter was far too pre-occupied with himself and his own concerns to notice anything strained or unusual in Vanderlyn's face. All he saw was that here at last was the man he wanted to see; his sulky face lightened, and he walked forward with hand outstretched.

"Hullo! Grid," he cried, "so here you are at last! You see I've not gone? There came a wire from the boy; he's hurt his knee-cap!"

Vanderlyn murmured an exclamation of concern; as they met he had wheeled round, thus avoiding the other's hand.

"Nothing much," went on Pargeter quickly, "but of course Peggy will be wild to go to him, so I thought I'd wait and take her to-morrow, eh! what?"

Side by side they began walking down the long reception-room. Vanderlyn was telling himself, with a feeling of sore, dull pain, that this was the first time, the very first time, that he had ever known Tom Pargeter show a kindly touch of consideration for his wife. But then this concerned the boy, of whom the father, in his careless way, was fond and proud; their child had always remained a link, if a slight link, between Tom and Peggy.

"It was just too late to get a wire through to her," went on Pargeter, fretfully, "I mean to that God-forsaken place where she's staying with Madame de Léra; but I've arranged for her to be wired to early in the morning. If I'd been half sharp I'd have sent the trolley for her——"

"The trolley?" repeated Vanderlyn, mechanically.

"The motor—the motor, man! But it never occurred to me to do it till it was too late."

"Would you like me to go out to-morrow morning and fetch her back?" asked Vanderlyn slowly.

"I wish you would!" cried the other eagerly, "then I should be sure of her coming back in time for us to start by the twelve-twenty train. When shall I send the trolley for you?"

"I'll go by train," said Vanderlyn shortly. "Madame de Léra's villa is at Marly-le-Roi, isn't it?"

"Yes, haven't you ever been there?"

Vanderlyn looked at Pargeter. "No," he said very deliberately, "I scarcely know Madame de Léra."

"How odd," said Pargeter indifferently. "Peggy's always with her, and you and Peggy are such pals."

"One doesn't always care for one's friends' friends," said Vanderlyn dryly. He longed to shake the other off, but Pargeter clung closely to his side. Each put on the hat and light coat handed to him; and, when once out on the boulevard, Pargeter slipped his hand confidingly through the other's arm.

His touch burnt Vanderlyn.

"By the way, Grid, I've forgotten to tell you why I wanted to see you to-night. I'd be so much obliged if you would go down to Chantilly at the end of the week and see how that new josser's getting on. You might drop me a line if everything doesn't seem all right."

Vanderlyn murmured a word of assent. This, then, was the reason why Pargeter had come to L'Union that night,—simply in order to ask Vanderlyn to keep an eye on his new trainer! To save himself, too, the trouble of writing a letter, for Tom Pargeter was one of those modern savers—and users—of time who prefer to conduct their correspondence entirely by telegram.

They were now close to the Place de l'Opéra. "Let's go on to 'The Wash,'" said Pargeter suddenly.

The eyes of the two men became focussed on the long line of brilliantly lit up windows of a flat overlooking the square. Here were the headquarters of a Paris club, bearing the name of America's first and greatest President, which had earned for itself the nickname of "Monaco Junior."

Tom Pargeter was no gambler,—your immensely wealthy man rarely is,— but it gave him pleasure to watch the primitive emotions which gambling generally brings to the human surface, and so he spent at what he called "The Wash" a good many of his idle hours.

"Let's turn in here for a minute," he said, eagerly, "Florac was holding the bank two hours ago; let's go and see if he's still at it."

Vanderlyn made a movement of recoil; he murmured something about having to be up early the next morning, but Pargeter, with the easy selfishness which so often looks like good-nature, pressed him to go in. "It's quite early," he urged again, and his companion was in no state of body or mind to resist even the slight pressure of another's will.

The brightly lighted rooms of "Monaco Junior" were full of colour, sound, and movement; the atmosphere was in almost ludicrous contrast to that of the decorous Union. The evening was only just beginning, the rooms were full, and Pargeter was greeted with boisterous warmth; here, if nowhere else, his money made him king.

He led the way to the card-room which, with its crowd of men surrounding each of the tables, was very evidently the heart of the club. "Do look at Florac!" he murmured to Vanderlyn. "When I left here a couple of hours ago, he was winning a bit, but I expect he's losing now. I always like to watch him play—he's such a bad loser!"

The two men had threaded their way close to the baccarat table, and now they formed the centre of a group who were throwing furtive glances at the banker, a pale lean Frenchman of the narrow-jowled, Spanish type so often repeated in members of the old noblesse.

The Marquis de Florac was "somebody," to use the expressive French phrase,—a member of that small Parisian circle of which each individual is known by reputation to every provincial bourgeois, and to every foreign reader of French social news.

There had been a time when de Florac had set the fashion, and that not only in waistcoats and walking-sticks. He was a fine swordsman, and was even now in some request as second at fashionable duels. None knew more certainly than he every punctilio of those unwritten laws which govern affairs of honour, and, had he been born to even a quarter of the fortune of Tom Pargeter, his record would probably have remained unstained. Unfortunately for him this had not been the case; he had soon run through the moderate fortune left him by his father, and he had ruined by his own folly, and his one vice of gambling, any chance that might have remained to him of a good marriage.

Even in the Faubourg St. Germain,—loyal to its black sheep as are ever the aristocracies of the old world,—Florac was now looked at askance; and in the world of the boulevards strange stories were told as to the expedients by which he now made—it could not be called earned—a living. The playing of those games which can best be described as requiring a minimum of judgment and a maximum of luck was apparently the only occupation remaining to the Marquis de Florac, and when in funds he was often to be found in the card-rooms of "Monaco Junior."

"He's losing now," whispered Pargeter. "I should think he's near the end of his tether, eh? Funny how money goes from hand to hand! I don't suppose Florac knows that it's *my* money he's chucking away!"

"Your money?" repeated Vanderlyn with listless surprise, "d'you mean to say that you've been lending Florac money?" He looked, with a pity in which there entered a vague fellow-feeling, at the mask-like face of the man against whom the luck seemed to be going so dead.

"I'm not quite a fool!" exclaimed Pargeter, piqued at the suggestion. "All the same, Grid, it *is* my money, or a little bit of it at any rate!"

An English acquaintance of the two men came up to them. "The French are a wonderful people," he said rather crossly, "everybody says that Florac is ruined,—that he's living on ten francs a day allowed him by a kind grandmother—and yet since I have been standing here he's dropped, at least so I've calculated, not far short of four hundred pounds!"

A grin came over Pargeter's small neat face, and lit up his odd, different-coloured eyes. "'*Cherchez la femme,*'" he observed, affecting an atrocious English accent; and then he repeated, as if he were himself the inventor, the patentee, of the admirable aphorism, "'*Cherchez la femme!* That's what you have got to do in the case of Florac, and of a good many other Frenchmen of his kind, I fancy!"

"I'm going home now, Pargeter," said Vanderlyn with sudden, harsh decision. "If you really wish me to go out to Marly-le-Roi in one of your cars to-morrow morning, will you please give orders for it to be round at my place at nine o'clock?"

V.

From what seemed an infinite distance, Vanderlyn awoke the next morning to hear the suave voice of his servant, Poulain, murmuring in his ear, "The automobile is here to take Monsieur for a drive in the country. I did not wish to wake Monsieur, but the chauffeur declared that Monsieur desired the automobile to be here at nine."

Poulain's master sat up in bed and stared at Poulain. Then suddenly he remembered everything that had happened to him the evening before. In a flash he even lived once more the wakeful hours of the night which had had so awful a beginning; only at four o'clock had he found sleep.

"Yes?" he said. Then again, "Yes, Poulain. I wished to start at nine o'clock. Say that I shall be down in a quarter of an hour."

"And then, while Monsieur is dressing, my wife will be preparing his little breakfast—unless, indeed, Monsieur would rather wait, and have his little breakfast in bed?"

"No," said Vanderlyn, quickly, "I shall not have time to wait for coffee."

The keen morning air, the swift easy motion of the large car revived Vanderlyn and steadied his nerves. He elected to sit in front by the side of Pargeter's silent English chauffeur. At this early hour the Paris streets were comparatively clear, and a few moments brought them to the Avenue du Bois de Boulogne. There, half way down was Tom Pargeter's splendid villa; as they passed it in a flash, Vanderlyn averted his head. To his morbid fancy it suddenly assumed the aspect of a great marble tomb.

The car swung on through the now deserted Bois; soon it was rushing up the steep countrified streets of St. Cloud, and then, settling down to a high speed, they found themselves in the broad silent alleys of those splendid royal woods which form so noble a girdle about western Paris. They sped through sunlit avenues of fresh green foliage, past old houses which had seen the splendid pageant of Louis the Fifteenth and his Court sweep by on their way to Marly-le-Roi, and so till they gained the lofty ridge which dominates the wide valley of the Seine.

Suddenly the chauffeur turned to Vanderlyn, and spoke for the first time: "Would you like to slow down a bit, sir? Mrs. Pargeter generally stops the car here to have a look at the view."

"No," said Vanderlyn hoarsely, "we haven't time to-day; we've got to get back to Paris in time for Mr. and Mrs. Pargeter to catch, if possible, the twelve-twenty o'clock train."

He leant back—a feeling of horror and self-contempt possessed him. His life was now one long lie; even when speaking to a servant, he was compelled to imply what he knew to be untrue.

They ran down into the quaint little town which has scarcely altered since the days when Madame du Barry was dragged hence, screaming and wringing her hands, to Paris, to prison, and to the guillotine. Vanderlyn's distraught imagination saw something sinister in the profound quietude of the place; it was full of shuttered villas, for through the winter each village in the neighbourhood of Paris hibernates, those whom the peasants style les bourgeois still regarding country life as essentially a summer pastime.

They now came to a high blank wall, broken by an iron gate. "This is the house, sir," said the chauffeur abruptly.

Vanderlyn jumped out, and rang a primitive bell; he waited some minutes and then rang again. At last he heard the sound of steps hurrying along a gravel path; and the gate was opened by an old woman.

"You have come to the wrong house," she said curtly, "this is Madame de Léra's villa." Then, as she caught sight of the Pargeters' chauffeur, a more amiable look stole over her wizened face,—"Pardon, perhaps Monsieur has brought a letter from Madame Pargeter?" She wiped her hand on her apron and held it out.

Vanderlyn remained silent a moment; he knew that now had come the moment for him to utter an exclamation of surprise, to explain that he had thought to find Mrs. Pargeter here,—but his soul revolted from the lie.

"Yes, I have come to see Madame de Léra," he said in a low voice. "Kindly give her my card, and ask her if she will be good enough to receive me?"

The old woman turned on her heel; she led Vanderlyn into the silent house, and showed him into a large sitting-room where the furniture was still swathed in the rough sheeting with which the careful French housewife drapes her household goods when leaving them for the winter.

"I will light the fire," said the servant, apologetically; "Madame does not use this room when we are here alone."

"I am quite warm," said Vanderlyn quickly. "Besides, I shall only be here a very few moments."

The woman gave him a curious, rather suspicious look, and went to find her mistress.

Vanderlyn, in spite of the words he had just uttered, suddenly told himself that, he felt cold—cold and dizzy. He moved over to the window. It overhung a wooded precipice, below which sparkled the Seine,—that same river into whose dark depths he had gazed so despairingly the night before. Here, looking at the sunlit panorama of wood, water, and sky spread out before him, Peggy must often have stood. For the first time since the terrible moment when he had watched the train bearing her dead body disappear into the darkness, Vanderlyn thought of her as living; he seemed to feel her soft, warm presence in this place which she had loved, and where she had spent peaceful, happy hours.

He heard the door open and shut, and, turning round, found himself face to face with the Frenchwoman whom he knew to have been Margaret Pargeter's devoted friend. Although he was well aware that Madame de Léra had never liked or trusted him, he, on his side, had always admired and appreciated her serenity and simple dignity of demeanour. As she came forward, clad in the austere dress of a French widow, he noted the expression of constraint, of surprise, on her worn face.

"Mr. Vanderlyn?" she said, interrogatively; and, as she waited for an explanation of the American's presence, surprise gave way to a look of great sternness and severity, almost of dislike. Nay more, Madame de Léra's attitude was instinct with protest—the protest of an honest woman drawn unwillingly into what she feels to be an atmosphere of untruth and intrigue. She was telling herself that she owed the fact of Vanderlyn's visit to some slight hitch in the plan in which she had been persuaded to play the part of an accomplice; she felt that Margaret Pargeter ought not to have subjected her to an interview with her lover.

Vanderlyn reddened. He felt suddenly angered. Madame de Léra's manner was insulting, not only to him, but—but to Mrs. Pargeter, to his poor dead love. Any thought of telling Madame de Léra the truth, or even part of the truth, left him.

"You must forgive my intrusion," he said, coldly; "I have come with a message from Mr. Pargeter. He believes his wife to be here, and he wishes her to be informed that her son, little Jasper, has had an accident. When the news arrived last night, it was too late to telegraph, and so he asked me to come here this morning in his motor in order to bring Mrs. Pargeter back to Paris. He proposes that she should accompany him to England to-day by the twelve o'clock train."

An expression of deep bewilderment crossed Madame de Léra's face. For the first time since she had glanced at Vanderlyn, she became aware that she was in the presence of a man who was suffering under some keen stress of feeling. She became oppressed with a great misgiving. What did his presence here this morning, his strange unreal words, signify? What was the inward meaning of this sinister comedy? It was of course clear that the secret elopement had not taken place. But then, where *was* Mrs. Pargeter?

She cast a long searching look at Laurence Vanderlyn. The American's face had become expressionless. He seemed tired, like a man who had not slept, but the look she thought she had surprised,—that look telling of the suppression of deep feeling, of hidden anguish,—had gone. The fact that she did not know how much Vanderlyn knew she knew added to Madame de Léra's perplexity. She was determined at all costs not to betray her friend.

"I regret to inform you," she said, quietly, "that Mrs. Pargeter is not here. It is true that I was expecting her to come yesterday. But she disappointed me— she did not come. Does no one know where she is?" She threw as great an emphasis as was possible in the impassive French language into her question.

Vanderlyn avoided her perplexed, questioning glance. "Since yesterday evening," he answered, "all trace of Margaret Pargeter has been lost. She seems to have left her house about six o'clock, and then to have disappeared—utterly. The servants believed," he added, after a pause, "that she was coming straight to you; she had, it seems, taken some luggage to the station the day before, and seen personally to its despatch."

There was a pause; neither spoke for some moments, and Madame de Léra noticed that Vanderlyn had not asked her if Peggy's luggage had arrived at her house.

"Then, Monsieur, it is surely clear," she exclaimed at last, "that there has been an accident, a terrible accident to our poor friend! I mean on her way to—to the station. But doubtless that thought has also occurred to you—if not to Mr. Pargeter—and you have already made all necessary enquiries?"

Vanderlyn, from being pale, flushed deeply. "No," he said, "I am afraid nothing of the kind has been done—yet. You see, Pargeter believes her to be here."

The words "But you—*you* knew she was not here!" trembled on Madame de Léra's lips, but she did not utter them. She felt as if she were walking amid quicksands; she told herself that there was far more danger in saying a word too much than a word too little.

"I regret," she said, "that you have made a useless journey, Mr. Vanderlyn. I must request you to go back and tell Mr. Pargeter that his wife is not here, and I beg, I entreat, you to inform the police that she is missing! For all we know,"—she looked at him with indignant severity,—"she may be lying ill, mortally injured, in one of our terrible Paris hospitals!"

As he made no assent to her imploring words, a look of anger came into Madame de Léra's eyes.

"I will ask you to allow me to return with you to Paris," she said, quickly. "I cannot rest inactive here in the face of the possibility, nay, the probability, I have indicated. If you, Mr. Vanderlyn, do not feel justified in making the enquiries I have suggested, no such scruple need restrain *me*."

She turned away, making no effort to mask her displeasure, almost her contempt, for the man who seemed to be so little moved by the mysterious disappearance of the woman he loved.

A few moments later Madame de Léra came back dressed for the drive. As they walked through into the hall of the villa, she suddenly turned, and with a strange gentleness asked her silent companion a question, "Mr. Vanderlyn, you look very tired; have you had any breakfast?"

He looked at her without answering, and she repeated her words.

"Yes," said Vanderlyn,—"that is, no, I have not. I was up late last night,— there was no time this morning," he spoke hurriedly, confusedly; the sudden kindness in her tone had brought scalding tears to his eyes, and he felt a nervous fear that he was about to break down. Madame de Léra took his arm; she opened a door and pushed him through into the kitchen, just now the one bright, warm, cheerful room in the house.

"My good Catherine," she said, "give this gentleman a cup of coffee— quickly!"

The presence of the old servant steadied Vanderlyn's nerves; with a muttered word of thanks he drank what was put before him, and then they went out, across the dewy lawn, to the gate.

Vanderlyn placed his companion in the back of the car, and himself took the vacant seat next to Pargeter's phlegmatic chauffeur, for he wished to remain silent. Madame de Léra's alteration of manner, her gentleness, her implied sympathy, frightened him. He would rather have endured her cold air of protest, of dislike.

And yet, as they drove swiftly back to Paris, taking, however, rather longer on the return journey, for the country roads were now full of animation and movement, Vanderlyn felt himself leaning, as against a wall, on Madame de Léra's strong upright nature. She might dislike, disapprove, even despise him,—but in this matter they would be one in their desire to shield Peggy's fair name. He would have given much to be able to still her evident anxiety, but that course was, so he felt, forbidden to him; he had no right to share with another human being the burden of his knowledge, of his awful grief. With a pang he reminded himself that even Madame de Léra's state of suspense was preferable to a knowledge of the truth.

At last they turned into the Bois de Boulogne, rushing through the leafy roads at a high speed; a few moments more would see them in the beautiful avenue where stood, isolated from its neighbours, the Villa Pargeter, instinct with flamboyant luxury and that perfection only achieved by the lavish use of money.

Tom Pargeter had a supreme contempt for the careless way in which the French millionaires of his acquaintance conducted their lives. He liked to get the full value of his money, and was proud of boasting to his intimates that he kept the people who worked for him up to the top mark. So it was that the sanded garden, even now blazing with flowers, which surrounded the square marble villa, and separated it from the carriage road and tan gallop, looked like a set piece, a vivid bit of scene painting, in the bright morning sunlight.

When they came within sight of the wrought bronze gates of the villa, Madame de Léra stood up in the car and leant over the front. She touched Vanderlyn on the shoulder. "Then if we find that Mr. Pargeter is still without any knowledge of his wife, I am to say that I know nothing—that I was expecting her yesterday evening, and that she never arrived?"

"Yes," he answered, "that is, Madame, what I expect to hear you say. It will then be for Mr. Pargeter to take what steps he judges proper."

As the powerful car swung through the gates, Vanderlyn saw that the front-door was wide open, and that the English butler was waiting to receive them; when the man saw that his mistress was not in the car, a look of perplexity came over his impassive face.

"Mr. Pargeter has been awaiting you, sir, for the last half hour," he said, "he is very anxious to catch the twelve o'clock express. The luggage has already gone on to the station. Mr. Pargeter wished the car to wait,—but—but is it to wait, sir?" he asked, helplessly.

"Yes," said Vanderlyn, shortly, "the car had better wait. Where is Mr. Pargeter?"

"He's not down yet, sir; he is breakfasting in his dressing-room. All the arrangements were made last night, but I will let him know you have arrived, sir." He looked doubtfully at Madame de Léra, too well trained to ask any question, and yet sufficiently human not to be able to conceal his astonishment at Mrs. Pargeter's non-appearance. Then, preceding the two visitors upstairs, he led them through the suite of large reception-rooms into a small octagon boudoir which was habitually used by Margaret Pargeter as her sitting-room.

There he left them, and, standing amid surroundings which all spoke to them, to the woman, of her friend, to the man of his love,—from the hooded chair where Peggy generally sat to the little writing-table where she had written so many notes to them both,—Madame de Léra and Laurence Vanderlyn felt overwhelmed with a common feeling of shame, of guilt. In silence they waited for Tom Pargeter, avoiding each other's eyes; and the Frenchwoman's fine austere face grew rigid—this was the first time in her long life that she had been connected with an intrigue. She felt humiliated, horrified at the part she now found herself compelled to play.

In spite of its costly luxury, and its wonderful beauty of decoration,—an exquisite Nattier was let into a panel above the fireplace, and a row of eighteenth-century pastels hung on the light grey walls,—the octagon apartment lacked the restful charm which belongs to many a shabby little sitting-room. The architect of the villa had sacrificed everything to the great reception-rooms, and in the boudoir were far too many doors.

One of these, which Vanderlyn had never noticed before, was now suddenly flung open, and, outlined against a narrow winding staircase, stood a figure which appeared at once grotesque and menacing to the man and woman who stood staring at the unexpected apparition. It was Tom Pargeter, clad in a bright yellow dressing-gown, and holding a fork in his left hand.

"I say, Peggy, look sharp,—there's no time to be lost! I told Plimmer to pack some of your things—not that there's any reason why you should come if you don't want to—for there's nothing much the matter with the boy, and he'll probably get well all the quicker if you——"

The speaker suddenly broke short the quick sentences; he stared round the little room, and then, catching sight of Madame de Léra who had been partly concealed by a screen, "Damn!" he said, and turning, scampered heavily up the staircase, leaving the door behind him open.

Vanderlyn and his companion looked at each other uncomfortably. Madame de Léra was not perhaps quite so shocked, either by Pargeter's appearance or by his one exclamation apparently addressed to herself, as the punctilious American supposed her to be. She knew no word of the English language, and in her heart regarded all foreigners as barbarians.

They waited,—it seemed a long, long time, but as a matter of fact it was but a very few minutes after Pargeter's abrupt entrance and exit, when his short quick steps were heard resounding down the long suite of reception-rooms. As he walked into the boudoir, the master of the house—this time dressed in a suit of the large checks he generally wore—bowed awkwardly to Madame de Léra, and then went over and shut the door giving access to the winding staircase, that which in his hurry he had omitted to close behind him. Then, and not till then, he turned to Laurence Vanderlyn.

"Well?" he said, "what's happened to Peggy? I'm told she's not here. Is she ill?"

"Peggy never arrived at Marly-le-Roi," said Vanderlyn.

To himself his very voice seemed changed, his words charged with terrible significance; but to Pargeter, the answer given to his question sounded disagreeably indifferent and matter-of-fact.

"Never arrived?" he echoed. "Where is she then? You don't mean to say she's lost?"

"Madame de Léra," said Vanderlyn, still in the same quiet, emotionless voice, "thinks that she's met with an accident,"—he looked imploringly at the Frenchwoman; surely it was time that she should come to his help. "I am telling Mr. Pargeter," he said to her in French, "that you fear she has met with an accident"

"Yes!" she exclaimed, eagerly turning to Pargeter, "how can it be otherwise, Monsieur?" She hesitated, looked at Vanderlyn, then quickly withdrew her eyes from his face. His eyes were full of agony. She felt as if she had peered through a secret window of another's soul.

"That is why I have come back to Paris," she went on, addressing Peggy's husband, "for I feel that not a moment should be lost in making enquiries. There are certain places where they take those who meet with accidents in our streets—accidents, alas! more and more frequent every day. Let us start at once and make enquiries."

Tom Pargeter heard her out with obvious impatience. But still his varnish of good breeding so far lasted that he muttered a word or two of gratitude for the trouble she had taken. Then he turned to Laurence Vanderlyn.

"Surely *you* don't think anything has happened to her, Grid?" he asked, nervously. "Now I come to think of it, she was a fool not to take one of the cars. Then we should have had none of this worry. I've always said the Paris cabs weren't safe. What d'ye think we had better do? We can't start out and make a round of all the hospitals—the idea's absurd!" Waiting a moment, he added dismally, "It's clear I can't take that twelve-twenty train."

He walked over to one of the windows, and drummed with his fingers on the pane.

Although Madame de Léra did not understand a word he said, Pargeter's attitude was eloquent of how he had taken the astounding news, and she looked at him with angry perplexity and pain. She said something in a low voice to Vanderlyn; as a result he walked up to Pargeter and touched him on the shoulder.

"Tom," he said, "I'm afraid something ought to be done, and done quickly. Madame de Léra suggests that we go to the Prefecture of Police; every serious accident is, of course, always reported there at once."

The other turned—"All right," he said, sullenly, "just as you like! But I bet you anything that after we have taken all that trouble, we shall come back to find Peggy, or news of her, here. You don't know her as well as I do! I don't believe she's had an accident; I daresay you'll laugh at me, Grid, but all I can say is that I don't *feel* she's had an accident. Take my word for it, old man, there's nothing to be frightened about. Why, you look quite pale!"

There came the distant sound of a telephone bell. "There!" he cried, "I expect that *is* Peggy, or news of her. What a bore it is having three telephones in a house!" He left the room, and a moment later they heard him shouting to his butler.

Vanderlyn turned to Madame de Léra. "He doesn't believe that Mrs. Pargeter has had an accident," he said, quietly, "you must not judge him too harshly." He added, after a moment, "I think you must know, Madame de Léra, that Mrs. Pargeter's husband has always been lacking in imagination."

Her only answer was a shrug of her shoulders.

VI.

Once a year the newspapers of each great capital publish, among other statistics, a record of the disappearances which have occurred in their midst during the preceding twelve months. These disappearances are not counted by tens or by hundreds, but by thousands; and what is true of every great city is in a very special sense true of Paris, the human Cloaca Maxima of the world. There, the sudden vanishing, the obliteration as it were, of a human being—especially of a foreigner—arouses comparatively little surprise or interest among those whose weary duty it is to try and find what has become of the lost one.

To Madame de Léra,—even to Tom Pargeter,—the beginning of what was to be so singular and perplexing a quest had about it something awe-inspiring and absorbing. So it was that during the few minutes which elapsed between their leaving the Avenue du Bois de Bologne and their reaching the ancient building where the Paris Police still has its headquarters, not a word was spoken by either of the two ill-assorted companions who sat together in the rear of the car, for Vanderlyn, the only one of the three who knew where the Prefecture of Police is situated, had been placed next to the chauffeur in order that he might direct him as to the way thither.

By such men as Tom Pargeter and their like, the possibility of material misfortune attacking themselves and those who form what may be called their appanage, is never envisaged; and therefore, when such misfortune comes to them, as it does sooner or later to all human beings, the grim guest's presence is never accepted without an amazed sense of struggle and revolt.

The news of the accident to his little son had angered Pargeter, and made him feel ill-used, but that it should have been followed by this mystery concerning his wife's whereabouts seemed to add insult to injury. So it was an ill-tempered, rather than an anxious man who joined Vanderlyn on the worn steps of the huge frowning building wherein is housed that which remains the most permanent and the most awe-inspiring of Parisian institutions.

As they passed through the great portals Tom Pargeter smiled, for the first time; "We shall soon have news of her, Grid," he murmured, confidently.

Vanderlyn winced as he nodded a dubious assent.

But at first everything went ill with them. Pargeter insisted on sending for the police interpreter and stating his business in English; then, irritated at the man's lack of comprehension, he broke out—to Vanderlyn's surprise—into voluble French. But as the two foreigners were sent from room to room in the old-fashioned, evil-smelling building, as endless forms were placed before them to be filled up, it became increasingly clear that the disappearance of a human being, especially of an Englishwoman, did not strike the listless employees as being particularly remarkable.

The more angry Pargeter grew and the more violent in his language, the more politely, listlessly, indifferent became those to whom he addressed his questions and indignant complaints.

The cosmopolitan millionaire-sportsman, accustomed to receive a constant stream of adulation and consideration from all those with whom life brought him in contact, was first amazed, and then angered, by the lack of interest shown in him and in his affairs at the Prefecture of Police.

Then, to his surprise and only half-concealed mortification, a reference made by Laurence Vanderlyn to an incident which had taken place the year before—that is, to the disappearance of an American citizen—followed by the production of the diplomatist's card, brought about a magic change.

Immediately the two friends were introduced into the presence of an important official; and a moment later Tom Pargeter's outraged dignity and sense of importance were soothed by an outpouring of respectful sympathy, while in an incredibly short time the full particulars of every accident which had occurred in the streets of Paris during the last twenty-four hours were laid before the anxious husband. But it soon became clear that in none of these had Mrs. Pargeter been concerned.

The official left the room a moment; then he returned with a colleague.

This man, the chief of the detective force, proceeded with considerable tact to examine and cross-examine both Pargeter and Vanderlyn concerning the way in which Mrs. Pargeter had spent the earlier part of the previous day— that is, the day on which she had disappeared.

The man's manner—that of scenting a secret, of suspecting that more lay behind the matter than was admitted by the husband and friend of the woman they were seeking—produced a disagreeable impression on Vanderlyn. For the first time he felt himself faced by a vague, but none the less real, danger, and the feeling braced him.

"Then Monsieur did not see this lady yesterday at all?"

"No," said Vanderlyn, shortly; "the last time I saw Mrs. Pargeter in her house was the day before yesterday, when I called on her about five o'clock."

"Monsieur is not related to the lady," asked the detective quietly.

"No," said Vanderlyn again. "But I am an old friend of both Mr. and Mrs. Pargeter, and that is why he asked me to accompany him here to-day."

"Then when and how did you yourself first learn of Madame Pargeter's disappearance?" asked the other suddenly.

Vanderlyn hesitated; for a moment his tired brain refused to act—when was he supposed to have heard of Peggy's disappearance? He looked helplessly at Pargeter, then said suddenly, "I met my friend at L'Union last night."

"Then you already knew of Madame's disappearance last night?" said the official eagerly.

"No! no!" exclaimed Pargeter crossly. "Of course we didn't know then! We didn't know till just now—that is, till this morning, when Mr. Vanderlyn went out to Madame de Léra's villa to fetch my wife. It was Madame de Léra who told us that she had never arrived at Marly-le-Roi. She disappeared yesterday afternoon, but we did not know it till this morning."

"May I ask you, gentlemen, to wait for a moment while I make certain enquiries?" observed the detective politely. "You have not yet been shown our daily report concerning the stations of Paris—is it not possible that Madame Pargeter may have met with some accident at the Gare St. Lazare, if, as I understand, she was going to her friend by train, and not by automobile?"

Pargeter seemed struck by the notion. He turned to Vanderlyn. "I can't make out," he said in a puzzled tone, "why Peggy thought of going to Marly-le-Roi by train when she might so easily have gone in her new motor."

"Peggy gave her man a week's holiday," said Vanderlyn shortly. "You know, Tom, that he wanted to go to his own home, somewhere in Normandy."

"Yes, yes. Of course! But still she might have gone out in the big car—I wasn't using it yesterday."

The detective came back at the end of what seemed to both Vanderlyn and Pargeter a very long quarter of an hour.

"No incident of any sort took place last night at the Gare St. Lazare," he said briefly. "We shall now institute a thorough enquiry among our agents; every police-station in Paris shall be notified of the fact that Madame Pargeter is missing; and I shall almost certainly be able to send you some kind of news of her by four o'clock this afternoon. In any case you can trust us to do our best. Will Monsieur be returning to the Avenue du Bois"—he addressed Vanderlyn, "or is Monsieur going to his own flat in the Rue de Rivoli?"

Vanderlyn looked up quickly. His private address was not printed on the card he had shown; still it was reasonable enough that this man should have looked up his own as well as Pargeter's address and should have wished to verify their statements as far as was possible.

"Of course, Grid, you will come home with me!" exclaimed Pargeter fretfully.

"Then, Messieurs, I will send any news I get straight to the Avenue du Bois de Boulogne."

As they walked through the long corridors, it became clear that whatever anxiety Pargeter had suffered had dropped off him, for the moment, like a cloak. "I shouldn't be surprised if I can get off to-night after all," he said cheerfully, "you heard what he said? This afternoon we shall certainly have news of her."

Then, as they emerged into the hall, and he caught sight of his motor-car and of its occupant, "For God's sake, Grid," he said frowning, "let's get rid of that old woman! There she sits, staring like a bird of prey; it's enough to give one the hump! Ask her if she would like us to drive her to her Paris house. If she wants to go back to the country, I'll send her in Peggy's Limousine—oh! I forgot, that's not available, is it? Never mind, she can go on in this car. Say we'll send her news as soon as we hear any!"

But Vanderlyn soon ascertained that Madame de Léra had no wish to go back to Marly-le-Roi. She accepted his brief account of what had occurred at the Prefecture of Police without comment, and, refusing Pargeter's offer to drive her to her house in the Faubourg St. Germain, asked only to be set down at the nearest telegraph-station.

Dreary hours followed—hours later remembered with special horror and shrinking by Laurence Vanderlyn. They were spent by the two ill-assorted friends in Tom Pargeter's own room on the ground-floor of the villa.

It was a long, well-lighted room, lined with the huge, splendidly decorative posters, signed Chéret and Mucha, which were then just being collected by those who admired that type of flamboyant art. In this apartment Peggy, as Vanderlyn was well aware, never put her feet, for it was there that her husband received his trainer and his sporting friends. Here also was his own private telephone.

Lunch was brought to them on a tray, and at two o'clock the butler came with the information that several police officials were in the house interrogating the servants. Far from annoying Pargeter, the fact seemed to afford him some gratification, for it proved that he was after all quite as important a personage as he believed himself to be. He gave orders that the men were to be liberally supplied with drink.

An hour later came a high official from the Préfecture. He was taken upstairs and shown into the drawing-room, and it was there that Pargeter joined him, leaving Vanderlyn for the first time alone.

The American lay back in the rocking-chair in which he had been sitting forward listening to the other's unconnected talk. What a relief, what an immense sense of sobbing relief—came over his weary senses, aye, even his weary limbs! He put away the thought, the anguished query, as to how long this awful ordeal was likely to endure. For the moment it was everything to be alone. He closed his smarting eyes.

Suddenly the telephone bell rang, violently. Vanderlyn got up slowly; stumblingly he walked across the room and took up the receiver. A woman's voice asked in French:

"Has Mr. Pargeter left Paris?"

"No," said Vanderlyn shortly. "Mr. Pargeter is still in Paris."

"Is it a friend of Mr. Pargeter who is speaking?"

There was a long pause,—then, "Yes," said Vanderlyn.

"Will you, Monsieur, kindly inform your friend," said the voice, shaking with a ripple of light laughter, "that Mademoiselle de la Tour de Nesle has something very urgent to say to him?"

"Mr. Pargeter is engaged, but I will give him any message."

"May I ask you, Monsieur, to have the gracious amiability to inform Mr. Pargeter that Mademoiselle de la Tour de Nesle will be expecting him at five o'clock this afternoon. She understood he was leaving Paris yesterday, but someone told her that he had been seen driving in his auto on the grand boulevards this morning."

A few moments later Pargeter burst into the room.

"They declare that Peggy must have left Paris!" he exclaimed. "I thought as much," he went on, angrily. "I felt certain that she was only hiding! Of course I didn't like to say so—at first," and, as Vanderlyn remained silent, he came and flung himself in a chair close to the other man.

"You see, Grid,"—his voice unconsciously lowered,—"she played me that trick once before—years ago! It was a regular bit of bad luck, the sort of thing that only seems to happen to me; other men escape. A woman came to our house,—we were living in London then,—an old friend of mine with whom I'd stupidly mixed up again; she brought a child with her, a squalling brat two or three months older than Jasper—Of course the child had nothing to do with me, but she said he had, and Peggy believed her!" he looked for sympathy to the silent man opposite to whom he was now sitting.

"Did you ever hear of this before?" he asked suspiciously, "did Peggy ever tell you about it?"

"No," said Vanderlyn. "This is the first time I have heard anything of it. How long did she stay away?" he forced himself to add, loathing himself the while: "Did she disappear like this—I mean, as she has done this time?"

"Well, not exactly," said Pargeter reluctantly, "for one thing she took Jasper and his nurse with her, but not her maid. They went off to her aunt,—the aunt who brought her up, you know,—but for two days I hadn't a notion where she was! Then one of her brothers came to see me. It was all made as damned unpleasant for me as possible, but they were of course determined that she should come back to me, and so she did—after about a week. But she was never nice to me again," he added, moodily, "not that she ever was really nice to me before we married. It was the aunt who hunted me——"

"Is there any special reason why Peggy should have thought of going away like that—now?" asked Vanderlyn in a strained voice.

"No," exclaimed Pargeter, "of course there isn't! I've always been nice to her, as you know well, Grid,—much nicer, I mean, than most men would have been to a wife who was so—so—" he sought intently for a word, "so superior and—and unsympathetic. But lately I have been specially nice to her, for my sister, Sophy, you know, had written me a long screed,—I didn't bother to read it right through, making out that Peggy's heart was weak, and that I ought to be very careful about her. The very day I got the letter I went out and bought her that grey Limousine Lady Prynne was so keen I should take off her hands! Peggy always had everything she wanted," he repeated; "I didn't have a penny with her, but I've never grudged her anything. In fact I should be pleased if she spent more on her clothes than she seems to care to do, for I like to see a woman well trigged out."

"Tom, I have a message for you," said Vanderlyn slowly, "a lady telephoned just now to say she's expecting you at five o'clock."

"Eh! what?" said Pargeter, his fair face flushing, "a lady? What lady? Did she give her name?"

"Mademoiselle de la Tour de Nesle," said Vanderlyn, with curling lip.

"Oh Lord! What a plague women are!" said the other, crossly. "Sometimes I think it's a pity God ever made Eve! Such impudence, her ringing up here! Still, she's an amusing little devil."

"Are you going to see her?" asked Vanderlyn, "because if so I think I had better be getting back to my place. You see, I've rather neglected my work to-day."

Something in the other's tone impressed Pargeter disagreeably.

"I say, don't be shirty!" he exclaimed, "I know you've had a lot of bother, and I'm awfully grateful to you, and so will Peggy be when she knows. I sha'n't make up my mind about going to see Nelly till the last minute——"

"Nelly?" repeated Vanderlyn, puzzled—"Who's Nelly?"

"You know, Grid,—the—the person who rang me up. I always call her Nelly. Her name's such a mouthful—still, it's Nelly's Tower, isn't it? See? Perhaps to-day as there's all this fuss on I'd better not go and see her, eh, Grid? I wish I was like you," he added, a little shamefacedly, "you're such a puritan. I suppose that's why Peggy's so fond of you. Birds of a feather, eh? what?" his manner grew sensibly more affectionate and confidential.

The two men smoked on in silence. Vanderlyn was trying to choose a form of words with which he could bid the other farewell; he longed with a miserable longing to be alone, but that first day's ordeal was not yet over.

"I can't face dinner here," said Pargeter suddenly, "let's go and dine at that new place, the Coq d'Or."

Vanderlyn lacked the energy to say him nay, and they went out, leaving word where they were to be found.

Le Coq d'Or was a reconstitution of what had been, in a now deserted suburban resort, a famous restaurant dedicated to the memory and cult of Rabelais. Vanderlyn had already been there with American friends, but to Pargeter the big room, with its quaint mediæval furnishings and large panels embodying adventures of Gargantua, was new, and for a moment distracted his mind from what was still more of a grievance than an anxiety.

But they had not long been seated at one of the narrow oak tables which were supposed to be exact copies of those used in a mediæval tavern, when Pargeter began to turn sulky. The maître d'hôtel of the Coq d'Or was not aware of how important a guest was honouring him that night, and for a few moments no attention was paid to the two friends.

"I say, this is no good!" exclaimed Pargeter angrily, "let's go somewhere else—to the Café de Paris."

"For God's sake, Tom," exclaimed Vanderlyn harshly, "sit down! Can't you see I'm tired out? Let's stay where we are."

"All right. But I can tell you that at this rate we sha'n't get anything till midnight!" Still Pargeter sat down again, and fortunately there soon came up a waiter who had known the great sportsman elsewhere; and a moment later he was absorbed in the amusing occupation of making out a careful menu from a new bill of fare.

During the long course of the meal, Vanderlyn listened silently to Pargeter's conjectures concerning Peggy's disappearance—conjectures broken by lamentations over the contretemps which had made it impossible for him to leave Paris that day. Absorbed as he was in himself and his own grievances, Pargeter was yet keenly aware when his companion's attention seemed in any way to wander, and at last there came a moment when, leaving his cup of black coffee half full, he pushed his chair away with a gesture of ill-temper.

"I'm afraid, Grid, all this must be an infernal bore for you!" he said; "after all, Peggy's not your wife—no woman has the right to lead you such a dance as she has led me to-day. Let's try to forget her for a bit; let's go along to 'The Wash'?"

Vanderlyn shook his head; he felt spent, worn out. He muttered that he had work to do, that it was time for him to turn in.

Each man paid his portion of the bill, and, as they went through the glass doors giving onto the Boulevard, Vanderlyn noticed that on each side of the entrance to the Coq d'Or a man was standing, sentinel-wise, as if waiting for someone to go in or come out.

For a moment the two friends stood on the pavement.

"Let's take a fiacre," said Pargeter suddenly, "and I'll drive you to your place." The warm spring weather had brought out a number of open cabs. They hailed one of these, and, as they did so, Vanderlyn noticed that the two men who had been standing at the door of the restaurant entered another just behind them.

When at last he found himself in his own flat, and at last alone, Vanderlyn stood for a few moments in his empty sitting-room. Terrible as had been the companioned hours of the day, he now feared to be alone. It was too early to go to bed—and he looked back with horror to the wakeful hours which had been his the night before. So standing there he told himself that an hour's walk—he had not walked at all that day—would quiet his nerves, prepare him for the next day's ordeal.

As he made his way down the broad shallow stairs, his mind seemed to regain its elasticity. He realised that it must be his business to keep fit. A greater ordeal than anything which had yet befallen him lay there—in front of him. Soon, perhaps to-morrow, the Prefecture of Police would connect the finding of a woman's dead body in the train which had left Paris for Orange the night before, with Mrs. Pargeter's disappearance.

It would be then that he would need all his strength and self-control. He remembered with a thrill of anger the curious measuring glance the head of the Paris detective force had cast on him that morning. He wondered uneasily how far he had betrayed himself.

Passing through the porte cochère, he noticed that the concierge was talking to a neat, stout little Frenchman with whose appearance he felt himself familiar. Vanderlyn looked straight at the man; yes, this was undoubtedly one of the two watchers who had been standing outside the door of the Coq d'Or.

Then he was being followed, tracked? The Paris police evidently already connected him in some way with the disappearance of Mrs. Pargeter?

Instead of crossing the road to the deserted pavement which bounds the gardens of the Tuileries, the American turned to the left, and became merged in the slowly moving stream of men and women under the arcades of the Rue de Rivoli. As he walked along he became conscious, and that without once turning round, that his pursuer was close behind; when he walked slowly, the other, as far as possible, did the same, and when he hurried on, he could hear the tap-tap dogging his footsteps through the crowd.

At last, finding himself opposite the Hotel Continental, Vanderlyn stopped and deliberately read over the bill of fare attached to the door of the restaurant. As he did so, the light of a large réverbère beat down on his face; from the human current sweeping slowly on behind him a man quietly detached himself, and, standing for a moment by the side of the American diplomatist, looked up into his face with a long deliberate stare.

VII.

The fact that he was being watched had a curious effect on Laurence Vanderlyn. It roused in him the fighting instinct which he had had to keep in leash the whole of that terrible first day of repression, save during the moments when he had been confronted with the head of the detective department at the Prefecture of Police.

As at last he walked on, now choosing deliberately quiet and solitary streets, the footsteps of his unknown companion echoed loudly behind him, and he allowed himself, for the first time since the night before, the cruel luxury of recollection. For the first time, also, he forced himself to face the knowledge that any hour might bring as unexpected a development as had been the prolonged presence of Pargeter in Paris. He realised that he must, if possible, be prepared, forearmed, with the knowledge of what had occurred after he had left the darkened railway carriage at Dorgival. News travels slowly in provincial France, yet, even so, the fact that the dead body of a woman had been found in a first-class carriage of the Paris demi-rapide must soon have become known, and made its way into the local press.

Out of the past there came to Vanderlyn the memory of an old-fashioned reading-room frequented by him long years before when he was studying in Paris.

The place had been pointed out to him by one of the professors at the Sorbonne as being by far the best lending library on the left side of the Seine; and there, in addition to the ordinary reading-room, was an inner room, where, by paying a special fee, one could see all the leading provincial papers.

In some such sheet,—for in France every little town has its own newspaper,—would almost certainly appear the first intimation of so sinister and mysterious a discovery as the finding of a woman's dead body in the Paris train.

Vanderlyn wondered if the library—the Bibliothèque Cardinal was its name—still existed. If yes, there was every chance that he might find there what was vital to him to know, both in order to rid himself of the obsessing vision which he saw whenever he shut his tired eyes, and also that he might be prepared for any information suddenly forwarded to Pargeter from the Prefecture of Police.

The next morning Vanderlyn was scarcely surprised to see the man who had shadowed him the night before lying in wait for him before the house.

The American measured the other's weary face and stout figure, and then he began quietly walking up the now deserted arcades of the Rue de Rivoli; with a certain grim amusement, he gradually increased his pace, and when at last he turned into the great court of the Louvre, and stood for a moment at the base of the Gambetta Monument, he assured himself that he had out-distanced his pursuer.

Striding quickly across the most historic of Paris bridges, he threaded the narrow, tortuous thoroughfares dear to every lover of old Paris, till he reached the Place St. Sulpice. There, forming one of the corners of the square, was the house wherein was housed the Bibliothèque Cardinal, looking exactly as Vanderlyn remembered its having looked twenty years before. Even the huge leather-bound books in the windows seemed to be the same as in the days when the future American diplomatist had been, if not a merry-hearted, then a most enthusiastic student, making eager acquaintance with "The Quarter."

He walked into the shop, and recognised, in the stout, middle-aged woman sitting there, the trim young bourgeoise to whom he had often handed a fifty centime piece in those days which seemed so distant as almost to belong to another life.

"Have you still a provincial paper room?" he asked, in a low tone.

"Yes," said the dame du comptoir, suavely, "but we have to charge a franc for admission."

Vanderlyn smiled. "It used to be fifty centimes," he said.

"Ah! Monsieur, that was long ago! There are ten times as many provincial papers now as then!"

He put the piece of silver on the counter. As he did so, he heard the door of the shop quietly open, and, with a disagreeable feeling of surprise, he saw the man, the detective he believed he had shaken off, come up unobtrusively to where he was standing.

Vanderlyn hesitated——Then he reminded himself that what he was about to do belonged to the part he had set himself to play: "Well, Madame," he said, "I will go through into your second reading-room and glance over the papers;" he forced himself to add, "I am anxious to find news of a person who has disappeared—who has, I fear, met with an accident."

The detective asked a question of the woman; he spoke in a low voice, but Vanderlyn heard what he said—that is, whether there was any other way out of the two reading-rooms except through the shop. On the woman's replying in the negative, he settled himself down and opened an illustrated paper.

Vanderlyn began systematically going through the provincial papers of the towns at which he knew the train was to stop after he had left it at Dorgival; and after the first uneasy quarter of an hour he forgot the watcher outside, and became absorbed in his task. To his mingled disappointment and relief, he found nothing.

It was of course possible that on the discovery of a dead body in a Paris train, the matter would at once be handed over to the Paris police; that would mean, in this case, that a body so found would be conveyed to the Morgue.

The thought that this might be so made Vanderlyn's heart quail with anguish and horror, and yet, if such a thing were within the bounds of possibility, had he not better go to the Morgue alone and now, rather than later in the company of Tom Pargeter?

As he passed out of the reading-room into the book-shop, and so into the square, he understood for the first time, how it was that he had made so foolish a mistake concerning the detective. The latter at once entered a fiacre which had evidently been waiting for him, and, as Vanderlyn plunged into the labyrinth of narrow streets leading from the Place St. Sulpice to Notre Dame, he could hear the cab crawling slowly behind him.

Well, what matter? This visit to the Morgue was also in the picture—in the picture, that is, of Laurence Vanderlyn, the kindly friend of Tom Pargeter, helping in the perplexing, the now agonising, search for Mrs. Pargeter.

But when at last he came in sight of the sinister triangular building which crouches, toad-like, under the shadow of the great Cathedral, Vanderlyn's heart failed him for the first time. If Peggy were indeed lying there exposed to the careless, morbid glances of idle sightseers to whom the Morgue is one of the sights of Paris, he felt that he could not trust himself to go in and look at her.

He stood still for a few moments, and then, as he was about to turn on his heel, he saw coming towards him from out of the door of the Morgue a figure which struck a note of tragedy in the bright morning sunshine. It was Madame de Léra, her eyes full of tears, her heart oppressed by the sights she had just seen.

"There are three poor people there," she said, in a low voice, "two men and a woman, but not, thank God! our friend. I wonder if it is possible that we are mistaken—that there was no accident, Monsieur Vanderlyn? But then, if so, where is she—why has she not written to me?"

He shook his head with a hopeless gesture, afraid to speak lest he should be tempted to share with her his agony and complicated suspense.

"If she were a Catholic," added Madame de Léra pitifully, "I should be inclined to think—to hope—that she had gone to a convent; but—but for her there was no such place of refuge from temptation——" her voice as she uttered the last word became almost inaudible; more firmly she added, "Is it not possible that she may have gone to England, to her child?"

"No," said Vanderlyn, dully, "she has not done that."

He took her to her door, and then, as he had promised Tom Pargeter to do, went to the Avenue du Bois, there to spend with Margaret Pargeter's husband another term of weary waiting and suspense.

That second day, of which the closing hours were destined to bring to Laurence Vanderlyn the most dramatic and dangerous moments connected with the whole tragic episode of Mrs. Pargeter's disappearance, wore itself slowly, uneventfully away.

Tom Pargeter, alternating between real anxiety, and an angry suspicion that his wife was in very truth only hiding from him, poured into the ears of this man, whom he now regarded rather as his friend than his wife's, every theory which might conceivably account for Peggy's disappearance. He took note of every suggestion made to him by the members of the now intensely excited and anxious household, for Margaret Pargeter's gentle personality and thoughtful kindness had endeared her to her servants.

When Plimmer, her staid maid, evolved the idea that Mrs. Pargeter, on her way to the station, might have stopped to see some friend, and, finding that friend ill, have remained to nurse her,—the suggestion so seized hold of Pargeter's imagination that he insisted on spending the afternoon in making a tour of his own and his wife's acquaintances. To Vanderlyn's anger and pain, the only result of this action on his part was that Mrs. Pargeter's disappearance became known to a large circle, and that more than one of the evening papers contained a garbled reference to the matter.

Meanwhile, or so Pargeter complained, the officials of the Prefecture of Police remained curiously inactive. They were quite certain, so they told the anxious husband, of ultimately solving the mystery, but it was doubtful if any news could be procured before the next day, for they were now directing their researches to the environs of Paris—a new theory now evolved being that Mrs. Pargeter, having hired a motor cab to drive her to Marly-le-Roi, had met with an accident or sinister misadventure on the way thither.

VIII.

At last the long day wore itself out, and Vanderlyn, in the late afternoon, found himself once more in his own rooms, alone. He only owed his escape to-night to the fact that two of Mrs. Pargeter's relations had arrived from England—one of her many brothers, and a woman cousin who was fond of her. They, of course, were spending the evening with Pargeter, and so the American had a respite—till to-morrow.

Having eaten his solitary dinner with a zest of which he felt ashamed, he was now in his study leaning back in an easy-chair, with a pile of unread papers at his side.

As he sat there, in the quiet, almost shabby room, which was so curiously different from the splendours of the Pargeter villa, there came over him a sense of profound and not unpleasing lassitude.

He looked back to the last forty-eight hours as to a long nightmare, broken by the few solitary walks he had forced himself to take. But for these brief periods of self-communing, he felt that his body, as well as his mind, would and must have given way. Peggy's husband had leant helplessly on him, and from the first moment he had been—so indifferent onlookers would have told you—the sympathetic, helpful witness of the various phases Tom Pargeter had lived through during those long two days.

For something like a week Vanderlyn had been living so apart from the world about him that he had known nothing, cared nothing, about what had gone on in that world. That very day an allusion had been made in his presence to some public event of importance of which he was evidently quite ignorant, and the look of profound astonishment which had crossed an Embassy colleague's face, warned him that he could not go on as he had been doing without provoking considerable, and far from pleasant, comment.

Putting out his hand, he took up the *New York Herald*—not the Paris edition, in which there was almost certain to be allusions to that which he wished for the moment to forget—but the old home paper which had arrived by that day's mail, and which had been carefully opened and ironed out by the faithful Poulain.

The newspaper was a little over a week old; it bore the date, April 28. What had he been doing on the twenty-eighth of April? and then with a rush it all came back to him—everything he wished for the moment to forget. It was on the afternoon of that day, the first warm spring day of the year, that they had been tempted, he and Peggy, to make their way down into the heart of Paris, to the solitary Place des Vosges. It was there, it was then, that they had together planned that which had brought him to his present dreadful pass.

Vanderlyn put the paper back on the table, and his face fell forward on his hands; was he fated never to be allowed to forget—not even for a moment?

It was with relief that he welcomed the interruption caused by the entrance of his servant bearing a card in his hand. "A gentleman has come and insists on seeing Monsieur."

Poulain spoke in a mysterious, significant tone, one that jarred on Vanderlyn's sensitive nerves. The disappearance of Mrs. Pargeter had become an engrossing, a delightful drama, not only to the members of the Pargeter household, but also to Poulain and his worthy wife; and it had been one of the smaller ironical agonies of Vanderlyn's position that he did not feel himself able to check or discourage their perpetual and indiscreet enquiries.

"I have already told you," he said sternly, "that I receive no one to-night. Even if Mr. Pargeter himself comes, you are to say that I am out!"

"I'm afraid Monsieur will have to receive this gentleman."

"Poulain!" exclaimed Vanderlyn sharply. "This won't do! Go at once and inform this gentleman, whoever he may be, that I can see no one to-night."

"I did say so," observed Poulain, in an injured tone, "I explained to him that you would see no one. I said you were out—he said that he would wait. Then, Monsieur, not till then, he handed me his card. If Monsieur will give himself the trouble of looking at it, I think he will receive the gentleman."

Vanderlyn took the card with an impatient movement. He glanced at it. "Why did you not tell me at once," he said roughly, "who this—this person was? Of course I must see the Prefect of Police."

More than once, Vanderlyn had had proof of the amazing perfection and grip of the great, the mysterious organisation, that oligarchy within a republic, which has always played a paramount rôle in every section of Parisian life. The American diplomatist had not lived in France all these years without unconsciously acquiring an almost superstitious belief in the omnipotence of the French police.

He got up and placed himself between the lamp and the door. He knew slightly the formidable official whose presence here surely indicated some serious development in what had now become a matter of urgent interest to many quite outside the Pargeter circle.

The two or three moments' delay—doubtless the zealous Poulain was engaged in helping the important visitor off with his coat—were passed by Vanderlyn in a state of indescribable nervous tension and suspense. He was glad when they came to an end.

And yet the Frenchman who came into Vanderlyn's sitting-room, making a ceremonious bow, would have suggested no formidable or even striking personality to the eyes of the average Englishman or American. His stout figure, clad in an ill-cut suit of evening clothes, recalled rather a Gavarni caricature than a dapper modern official, the more so that his round, fleshy face was framed in the carefully trimmed mutton-chop whiskers which remain a distinguishing mark of the more old-fashioned members of the Parisian Bar. The red button, signifying that its wearer is an officer of the Legion of Honour, was exceptionally small and unobtrusive. Vanderlyn was well aware that his visitor was no up-start, owing promotion to adroit flattery of the Republican powers; the Prefect of Police came of good bourgeois stock, and was son to a legal luminary who had played a considerable part in '48. His manner was suave, his voice almost caressing in its urbanity——

"I have the honour, have I not, of speaking to Mr. Laurence Vanderlyn?"

Vanderlyn bowed; he turned and led the way to the fireplace. "Yes, Monsieur le Préfet, Laurence Vanderlyn at your service. I think we have already met, at the Elysée——" he drew forward a second armchair.

Monsieur le Préfet sat down; and for the first time the American diplomatist noticed that his visitor held a small, black, battered portfolio in his right hand. As the Frenchman laid it across his knee, he gave a scarcely perceptible glance round the room; then, at last, his gaze concentrated itself on the table where stood the lamp, and the spread-open newspaper.

"You probably divine, Monsieur," said the Prefect, after a short pause, "what has brought me here to-night. I have come to see you—perhaps I should say to consult you—in connection with the disappearance of Mrs. Pargeter."

"Yes?" said Vanderlyn interrogatively, "I am, of course, quite at your disposal. I have been with Mr. Pargeter all to-day, but so far the mystery remains as great as ever." He stopped abruptly, feeling it wisest not to speak, but to listen.

"That, I repeat, is why I have come here," said Vanderlyn's formidable visitor. He spoke with a great deliberateness and mildness of manner. "I cannot help thinking, my dear sir, that with your help we may be, or rather *I* may be, on the eve of a discovery."

Vanderlyn looked surprised; his desolate eyes met the older man's hesitating glance quite squarely, but this time he remained silent.

The Prefect went on speaking, and his voice became more and more suave; he was certainly desirous of saving in every way his host's susceptibilities.

"The fact that I have taken the very unusual course of coming myself to see you, Mr. Vanderlyn, will prove to you the importance I attach to this interview. Indeed, I wish to be quite frank with you——"

Vanderlyn bent his head, and then he sat up, listening keenly while the other continued——

"This is not, I am convinced, an ordinary case of disappearance, and it is to us, and especially to me, disagreeably complicated by the fact that the lady is an English subject and that her husband is a well-known and highly thought of member of our English colony. This makes me the more anxious to avoid"—he hesitated, then firmly uttered the two words, "any scandal. It was suggested at the Préfecture to-day that it would be well to make a perquisition, not only in Mrs. Pargeter's own house, but also in the houses of some of her intimates. Mr. Pargeter, as you know, gave the police every possible facility. Nothing was found in the Villa Pargeter which could throw any light on Mrs. Pargeter's disappearance. Now, Monsieur, before subjecting *you* to such an unpleasant occurrence, I decided to approach you myself——"

Vanderlyn opened his lips, and then closed them again.

"I have come to ask you, Monsieur, one question, and I give you my word as an honest man that what you tell me shall be treated as confidential. I ask you if you know more of this mysterious matter than you are apparently prepared to divulge? In a word—I beg you to tell me where Mrs. Pargeter is hiding at the present moment? I have no wish to disturb her retreat, but I beg you most earnestly to entrust me with the secret."

Again the speaker's eyes took a discreet journey round the plain, now shadow-filled room; his glance rested on the book-shelves which formed so important a part of its decorations, lingered doubtingly on a carved walnut chest set between two of the windows, peered through these same unshuttered windows on to the dark stone balconies, then, baffled, his eyes came back and fixed themselves on the American diplomatist's face.

A feeling of indescribable relief stole over Vanderlyn's wearied and yet alert senses. It was clear that the Prefect of Police knew nothing of the truth; the directness of his question proved it. Yet, even so, Vanderlyn felt that he must steer his way very warily.

"You are in error," he said at last, "for you credit me, Monsieur le Préfet, with a knowledge I do not possess."

"Ah!" said the other mildly, "that is most unfortunate!"

"May I, on my side, put to you a question to which I should be glad of an honest answer?" said Vanderlyn abruptly. "Are you now engaged in making a wide-spread enquiry among those who had the honour of this lady's acquaintance?"

"No, Monsieur,"—the Prefect's manner showed an eager desire to be quite frank,—"I am confining my personal enquiries to only two persons; that is, to a certain Madame de Léra, to whom you will remember Mrs. Pargeter was about to pay a visit at the moment she disappeared, and to yourself."

Vanderlyn made a sudden nervous movement, but he checked the words which rose to his lips, for the Prefect was again speaking, and this time with a certain excitement of manner.

"I am convinced that Mrs. Pargeter never intended to go to Madame de Léra, and that the proposed visit was a blind! The facts speak for themselves. Madame de Léra had taken only one servant to the country, and this servant, an old woman whom she has had with her many years, and whom she can entirely trust, had no idea that her mistress was expecting a visitor! I repeat—that no preparations for Mrs. Pargeter's arrival had been made at Marly-le-Roi. It is my belief—nay, my conviction—that Madame de Léra knows perfectly well where her friend is now concealed."

It was then that Vanderlyn committed what was perhaps the only mistake he was destined to commit during this difficult interview. "Has Madame de Léra made any such admission?" he asked quickly.

"No," answered the Prefect, looking at him thoughtfully, "Madame de Léra has made no admission; but then I have learned, through long experience, never to believe, where there is a friend in the case, what a lady tells me. Women of the world, my dear sir, are more loyal the one to the other than we men may choose to believe!"

"And men, Monsieur? Are they more disloyal?" Vanderlyn spoke quietly, indifferently, as if the question was of no moment.

"Men," said Monsieur le Préfet, dryly, "are as a rule quite as loyal, especially where they feel their honour is engaged. But with a man it is possible to reason; a woman, especially a good woman, follows the dictates of instinct,— in other words, of her heart."

"I notice, Monsieur le Préfet, that you eliminate the possibility of material accident having occurred to Mrs. Pargeter?"

"Let us distinguish!" exclaimed the older man quickly. "If, by accident, you mean, Mr. Vanderlyn, the type of mishap which might have occurred to this lady when she was walking or driving in our Paris streets, then I certainly eliminate the possibility of accident to Mrs. Pargeter. Within six hours of such a thing having occurred the facts would have been laid before me, and, as you know, two nights and two days have elapsed since her disappearance.

If, on the other hand, we envisage the possibility of suicide, then are opened up a new series of possibilities."

The Prefect gave a piercing look at the American's worn and sorrow-laden face, but he did not find written there any involuntary answer to his mute interrogation.

"Some years ago," went on the great official, "a man well known in Paris society made up his mind to take his own life. He hired a cellar, locked the door, and then shot himself. Months went by before his disappearance was accounted for, and then the body was only discovered by an accident. If Mrs. Pargeter has committed suicide, and if she, an intelligent woman, was determined that the fact should never be found out by her friends, then I admit our task becomes a very difficult one! But I do not believe," he continued, after a short silence, "that Mrs. Pargeter did this. I believe she is alive, and well. She was, by each account that has reached me, young, charming, and wealthy. She had a child whom she apparently adored. As for her relations with her husband——" the Prefect shrugged his shoulders, and again looked searchingly at Vanderlyn.

"Mr. Thomas Pargeter," he went on, smiling, "is not perhaps the perfect husband of whom every young girl dreams; but then no one is so foolish as to search for the perfect husband in the world to which your friend belongs! He is not exactly a *viveur*,—but he is, to use the slang of the day, essentially a *jouisseur*. Is not that so?" He added, with a rather twisted grin, "If every lady whose husband lives to enjoy himself were to commit suicide, there would be very few women left in our Paris world."

"I agree with you, Monsieur le Préfet, in thinking Mrs. Pargeter was the last woman in the world to commit suicide," said Vanderlyn brusquely, and then he got up.

There had come over him during the last few moments an inexplicable, instinctive feeling of dread,—that panting fear which besets the hunted creature. He was determined to bring to an end the interview. But the Prefect of Police had no intention of being disposed of so easily. He remained sitting where he was; and, placing his two fat hands firmly on his knees, sat looking at the American's tall figure. Slowly his eyes travelled up till they rested on his host's haggard face.

"Then I am to understand, Mr. Vanderlyn, that you are not in a position to give me any help? That is your last word?"

Vanderlyn suddenly determined to carry the war into the enemy's country.

"I can only repeat," he said, harshly, "what I said before, Monsieur le Préfet—namely, that you credit me with a knowledge which I do not possess.

Further, that while, of course, I appreciate the kindly motive which has inspired your visit, I think I have a right to resent the suspicions which that visit indicates, I do not say on your part, but on that of your subordinates. I will not disguise from you my knowledge that for the last two days every step I have taken has been dogged; I suspect also, but of that I have no proof, that my servants, and the concierge of this house, have been questioned as to my movements, as to my daily life. I cannot help also suspecting—perhaps in this I am wrong—that the police are inclined to believe that Mrs. Pargeter—a woman, let me remind you, Monsieur le Préfet, of the highest and most unspotted character—is hiding here, in my chambers! You speak of having saved me from a perquisition,—a perquisition in the rooms of a diplomatist is a serious matter, Monsieur le Préfet, and I tell you quite frankly that I should have resisted such an outrage in every way in my power! But now, in the present very peculiar circumstances, I request,—nay, I demand,—that you should search my rooms. Every possible facility shall be afforded you." Vanderlyn's voice was shaking with undisguised anger,—aye, and disgust.

The Prefect of Police rose from his chair.

"I have no wish to subject you to any indignity," he said earnestly, "I absolutely accept your assurance that Mrs. Pargeter is not in hiding here. I am aware, Mr. Vanderlyn, that Americans do not lie,"—an ironic smile wavered for a moment over his large mouth.

Vanderlyn's face remained impassive. "You, on your side, must forgive my heat," he said, quietly. Then he suddenly determined to play for a high stake. "May I ask you to satisfy my curiosity on one point? What made you first suspect such a thing? What led you to—to suppose——"

"——That you knew where this lady was; that she might—say, after a little misunderstanding with her husband—have taken refuge with you? Well, yes, Mr. Vanderlyn, I admit that you have a right to ask me this, and it was because I feared you might lack the exquisite courtesy you have shown me, that I brought with me to-night a document which contains, in what I trust you will consider a discreet form, an answer to your delicate question."

Vanderlyn's visitor again sat down; he laid open on his knee the leather portfolio, and out of it he took a large sheet of foolscap, which, unfolding, he handed to Laurence Vanderlyn.

"This, Monsieur, is your *dossier*. If you can prove to me that it is incorrect in any particular, I will see that the error is rectified. We naturally take special care in compiling the *dossiers* of foreign diplomatists, for experience has shown that these often become of great value, even after the gentlemen in question have left Paris for some other capital."

Vanderlyn reddened. He glanced over the odd-looking document with eager, curious eyes. A few words here and there were printed, but the rest of the *dossier* was written in the round copying character which must be mastered by every French Government clerk hoping for promotion.

First came the American diplomatist's Christian name and surname, his place of birth, his probable age—right within two years,—a short epitome of his diplomatic career, a guess at his income, this item considerably under the right figure, and evidently based on his quiet way of living.

Then, under a printed heading "General Remarks," were written a few phrases in a handwriting very different from the rest—that is, in the small clear caligraphy of an educated Frenchman. Staring down at these, Vanderlyn felt shaken with anger and disgust, for these "General Remarks" concerned that part of his private life which every man believes to be hidden from his fellows:—

"Peu d'intimités d'hommes. Pas de femmes: par contre, une amitié amoureuse très suivie avec Madame (Marguerite) Pargeter. Voir dossier Pargeter (Thomas)."

Amitié amoureuse? Friendship akin to love? The English language, so rich in synonyms, owns no exact equivalent for this French phrase, expressive though it be of a phase of human emotion as old as human nature itself.

Vanderlyn looked up. His eyes met squarely those of the other man.

"Your staff," he said, very quietly, "have served you well, Monsieur; my *dossier* is, on the whole, extraordinarily correct. There is but one word which I would have altered, and which, indeed, I venture to beg you to correct without loss of time. The young man—he is evidently a young man—who wrote the summary to which you have drawn my attention, must have literary tastes, otherwise there is one word in this document which would not be there." Vanderlyn put his finger down firmly on the word "amoureuse." "My relations with Mrs. Pargeter were, it is true, those of close friendship, but I must ask you to accept my assurance, Monsieur le Préfet, that they were not what the writer of this passage evidently believed them to have been."

"I will make a note of the correction," said the Prefect, gravely, "and I must offer you my very sincere excuses for having troubled you to-night."

As Vanderlyn's late visitor drove home that night, he said to himself, indeed he said aloud to the walls of the shabby little carriage which had heard so many important secrets, "He knows whatever there is to be known—but, then, what is it that is to be known? Of what mystery am I now seeking the solution?"

IX.

As he heard the door shut on the Prefect of Police, Vanderlyn felt his nerve give way. There had come a moment during the conversation, when, as if urged by some malignant power outside himself, he had felt a sudden craving to take the old official into his confidence, and tell him the whole truth—so magnetic were the personality, the compelling will, of the man who had just left him.

He walked over to the corner window of his sitting-room, and stepped onto the stone balcony which overlooked the twinkling lights of the Place de la Concorde.

Then, flung out, merged in the deep roar below, there broke from Laurence Vanderlyn a bitter cry; the keen night air had brought with it a sudden memory of that moment when he had opened the railway carriage door and stepped out into the rushing wind.... He asked himself why he had not followed his first impulse, why he had not allowed himself to die, with Peggy in his arms? Why, above all, had he undertaken a task which it was becoming beyond his strength to carry through?

So wondering, so questioning, he leaned over the balustrade dangerously far; then he drew quickly back, and placing his hands on the parapet, stood for a moment as if holding at bay an invisible, yet to himself most tangible, enemy.

With a sigh which was a groan, he walked back into the room. He had never yet failed Peggy; he would not fail her now——

Vanderlyn sat down; he was determined not to be beaten by his nerves. He took up the *New York Herald*; but a moment later he had laid the paper down again on the table. What had been going on in America a week ago could not compel his attention. He took another paper off the table; it was the London *Daily Telegraph*, of which one of the most successful features for many years has been a column entitled "Paris Day by Day,"—an *olla podrida* of news, grave and gay, domestic and sensational, put together with infinite art, and a full understanding of what is likely to appeal to the British middle-class reader. There, as Vanderlyn knew well, was certain to be some reference to the disappearance of Mrs. Pargeter.

Yes—here it was!

"No trace of Mrs. Pargeter, the wife of the well-known sportsman and owner of Absinthe, has yet been found; but the lady's relations think it possible that she went unexpectedly to stay with some friends, and that the letter informing her household of her whereabouts has miscarried."

The Paris correspondent of the great London newspaper had proved himself very discreet.

Vanderlyn's eyes glanced idly down the long column of paragraphs which make up "Paris Day by Day." Again he remembered the look of deep astonishment which had crossed a colleague's face at his ignorance of some new sensation of which at that moment all Paris was apparently talking. So it was that he applied himself to read the trifling items of news with some care, for here would be found everything likely to keep him in touch with the gossip of the day.

At last he came to the final paragraph—

"Yet another railway mystery! The dead body of a woman has been found in a first-class compartment in a train which left Paris at 7 P. M. last Wednesday. As the discovery was not made till the train reached Orange, it is, of course, impossible to know where the unfortunate woman, who, by her dress, belonged to the leisured class, entered the train. Her hand baggage had disappeared, no doubt stolen at some intervening station by someone who, having made the gruesome discovery, thought it wise to make himself scarce. The police do not, however, consider that they are in the presence of a crime. Dr. Fortoul, the well-known physician of Orange, has satisfied himself that the lady died of heart disease."

Vanderlyn went on staring down at the printed words. They seemed to make more true, more inevitable, the fact of Margaret Pargeter's death, and of his own awful loss.

But with the agony of this thought came infinite relief, for this, or so he thought, meant that his own personal ordeal was at last drawing to a close. The fact of so strange and unwonted an occurrence as the finding of a woman's dead body in a train, would surely be at once connected by the trained intellects of the Paris Police with the disappearance of Mrs. Pargeter.

He let the paper fall to the ground and began to think intently. When that came to pass, as it certainly must do within the next few hours, it would become his grim business to persuade Tom Pargeter that the clue was one worth following. The mystery solved, the question of how Margaret Pargeter came to be travelling in the demi-rapide would be comparatively unimportant—at any rate not a point which such a man as Tom Pargeter would give himself much trouble to clear up.

Then with some uneasiness he remembered that before such an item of news could have found its way into an English newspaper, the fact must have been known to the French police for at least twelve hours. If that were so, their acumen was not as great as that with which Vanderlyn credited them.

But stay! The Prefect of Police was convinced that Mrs. Pargeter was alive, and that he, Vanderlyn, knew her whereabouts; it was not for Peggy dead, but for Peggy living, that they were still searching so eagerly.

He opened the *Figaro* and the *Petit Journal,* and ran a shaking finger down the columns; there, in each paper, hidden away among unimportant items, and told more briefly and in much balder language, he at last found the story of the discovery which the *Daily Telegraph* had served up as a tit-bit to thrill the readers of its Paris news columns.

Vanderlyn made up his mind to spend the whole of the next day with Pargeter; he must be at the villa, ready to put in his word of advice,—even, if need be, of suggestion,—when the moment came for him to do so.

For the first time for many nights Vanderlyn's sleep was unbroken; and early the next morning he made his way to the Avenue du Bois de Boulogne.

As he walked through the hall of the villa, already peopled with a score of the Pargeters' acquaintances, eager to show their sympathy with the wealthy sportsman in this most untoward and extraordinary occurrence, the American was obliged to shake hands with many men whom he had hitherto only known by sight, and to answer questions some of which impressed him as strangely indiscreet. More than one of those with whom he found himself thus face to face looked at him with cruel, inquisitive eyes, and a scarcely veiled curiosity, for it was of course well known that Laurence Vanderlyn had been an intimate, not only of the husband, but also of the wife.

At last Pargeter's valet threaded his way up to him: "Will you please come upstairs, sir? Mr. Pargeter told me to say that he would be glad if you would go to his dressing-room as soon as you arrived."

"There's no news, Grid,—no news at all! It's getting awful, isn't it?—quite beyond a joke! You know what I mean—I'm sick of answering stupid questions. I was waked this morning at seven—had to see a man in bed! They don't seem to understand that I can tell them nothing beyond the bare fact that she's vanished; they actually sent two women here last night——"

"Two women?" echoed Vanderlyn. "What sort of women?"

"Ugly old hags," said Pargeter, briefly, "from the Prefecture of Police. They brought an impudent letter asking me to allow them to turn out Peggy's room and look over all her things! But I refused——" he looked at his friend for sympathy—and found it.

"You were quite right," said Vanderlyn quickly. His face became rigid with anger and disgust. "Quite right, Tom! Whatever made them think of suggesting such a thing? Where would be the use of it?"

"Oh! well, of course they had a reason. The police are particularly keen that we should look over any old letters of hers; they think that we might find some kind of clue. But I don't believe she kept her letters—why should she? I don't keep mine. However, I've promised to do the job myself——" he looked uncertainly at Vanderlyn. "Would you mind, Grid, coming with me into Peggy's room? Of course Plimmer, that's her maid, you know, will help us. She knows where Peggy keeps all her things."

"Why not ask Madame de Léra to do it?" said Vanderlyn, in a low voice.

He turned away and stared at a sporting print which hung just on the level of his eyes. Had he ever written imprudent letters to Peggy? Not lately, but in the early days,—in that brief time of uncertain ecstasy, and, on his part, of passionate expression, which had preceded their long successful pretence at friendship? He himself had preserved later letters of hers—not love-letters assuredly, but letters which proved clearly enough the strange closeness of their intimacy.

But what was this that Pargeter was saying? "Madame de Léra? Why should I ask her to interfere? I don't want to mix her up in this business more than I can help! If it hadn't been for her—and that ridiculous invitation of hers, Peggy would be here now! Peggy wouldn't mind your looking over her things, Grid. She's really fond of you—as fond of you as she can be of anyone, that is."

He got up, and, preceding Vanderlyn down a connecting passage, flung open the door giving access to a spacious airy bedchamber of which the pale mauve and grey furnishings reminded both men of Peggy's favourite flower and scent. The sun-blinds were down and the maid was standing, as if waiting for them, by the dressing-table.

They both instinctively hesitated on the threshold. "Tom," said Vanderlyn, hoarsely, "I don't think I ought to come in here——"

"Don't be a fool! I tell you she wouldn't mind a bit. Surely you're not going to cut—now?"

Pargeter took a step forward; then he stood for a moment looking round him, evidently perplexed, and ill at ease at finding himself thus suddenly introduced into his wife's intimate atmosphere.

"I don't believe she kept any letters," he repeated, then glanced uncertainly at the lady's-maid who stood primly by.

"Mrs. Pargeter kept some letters in that writing-desk over there, sir,—at least I think she did."

Close to the small tent-bed stood an old-fashioned rosewood davenport, a relic of Margaret Pargeter's childhood and girlhood, brought from her distant English home.

The maid waited for a moment, and then added, "The desk is locked, sir."

"Locked? Then did Mrs. Pargeter take her keys with her?"

"I suppose she did, sir."

"Then it's no use," said Pargeter, with a certain relief, "I don't want to force the thing open."

Vanderlyn looked across, coldly and steadily, at the woman. Her expression struck him as oddly enigmatical; meeting his glance, Plimmer reddened, her eyes dropped. "I expect any simple key would open it," he said, briefly.

"Well, sir, I did ask the housekeeper to lend me a bunch of keys. Here they are," she opened one of the dressing-table drawers. "Perhaps one of the smaller ones would fit the lock."

It was Vanderlyn who took the keys from her strangely reluctant hand, and it was he who at last felt the old-fashioned lock yield.

"Now, Pargeter," he said, sharply, "will you please come over here?"

The whole of the inside of the desk was filled with neat packets, each carefully tied up and docketed; on several had been written, "In the case of my death, to be burnt;" on other packets, "To be returned to Madame de Léra in case of my death."

Vanderlyn saw that here at least were none of his letters, and none from Peggy's child.

"It's no use bothering about any of these," said Pargeter, crossly, "they can't tell us anything. Why anyone should trouble to keep old letters is quite beyond me!"

"That little knob that you see there, sir," said Plimmer, in her diffident, well-trained voice, "is the head of a brass pin; if you draw it out, sir, it releases the side drawer. I think you will find more letters there,—at least that is where Master Jasper's letters are, I know."

She looked furtively at Vanderlyn, and her look said, "If you want to have the truth you shall have it!"

"I say, how queer!" exclaimed Pargeter. "A secret drawer! eh, Grid?"

"All old pieces of furniture have that kind of thing," said Vanderlyn, "there isn't any secret about it."

Pargeter fumbled at the brass-headed pin; he pulled it out, and a drawer which filled up the side of the davenport shot out. Yes, here were more packets inscribed with the words, "Jasper's letters, written at school," and then others, "To be returned to Laurence Vanderlyn in case of my death;" and two or three loose letters.

"Well, these won't tell us anything, eh, Grid?" Pargeter opened the first envelope under his hand:—

DEAR MAMMY, (he read slowly),

Please send me ten shillings. I have finished the French cherry-jam. I should like some more. Also some horses made of gingerbread. I have laid 3 to 1 on Absinthe. Betting is forbidden, but as it was Dad's horse I thought I might. My bat is the best in the school.

Your lovingJASPER.

"He's a fine little chap, isn't he, Grid?" Pargeter was fingering absently a yellowing packet of Vanderlyn's letters: "Fancy keeping your old letters! What a queer thing to do!"

Vanderlyn said nothing. The maid stared at him stealthily.

At last Pargeter put the packet down, and deliberately opened yet another envelope which lay loose. "I suppose this is the last note you wrote to her?" he said, then, opening it, murmured its contents over to himself:—

DEAR PEGGY,

I hear the show at the Gardinets is worth seeing. I'll call for you at two to-morrow.

Yours sincerely,L. V.

"Well, it's no use our wasting any more time here, is it? We'd better go downstairs and have a smoke. Why—why, Grid!—what's the matter?"

"It's nothing," said Vanderlyn, roughly, "I'll be all right in a minute or two——"

"I don't wonder you're upset," said the other, moodily. "But just think what it must be for *me*. I can't stand much more of it. It's been simply awful since Peggy's brother and that cousin of hers arrived. They treat me as if I were a murderer! They're at the Prefecture of Police now, making what they're pleased to call their own enquiries."

They had left Peggy's room, and as he spoke Pargeter was leading the way down a staircase which led into his smoking-room.

Once there, he shut the door and came and stood close by Vanderlyn.

"Grid," he said, lowering his voice, "I've been wondering—don't you think it would be a good plan if I were to go and see that fortune-teller of mine, Madame d'Elphis? I don't mind telling you that I'd a shot at her yesterday evening, but she was away. She does sometimes make mistakes, but still, she's a kind of Providence to me. I never do anything important—I mean at the stables—without consulting her."

Vanderlyn looked at the eager face, the odd twinkling green and blue eyes, with scarcely concealed surprise and contempt.

"Surely you don't think she could tell you where—what's happened to Peggy?" he said incredulously.

"If I could have seen her last night," went on Pargeter, "I'd have got away to England to-day. There's no object in my staying here; *I* can't help them to find Peggy. But La d'Elphis won't see me before to-morrow morning. If she can't clear up the mystery nobody can. I'm beginning to think, Grid"—he came close up to the other man,—"that something must have happened to her. I'm beginning to feel—worried!"

X.

An hour later Vanderlyn had escaped from Pargeter, and was standing alone in Madame de Léra's drawing-room.

He was scarcely conscious of how many hours he had spent during the last terrible three days, with the middle-aged Frenchwoman who had been so true and sure a friend of Margaret Pargeter. In Madame de Léra's presence alone was he able, to a certain extent, to drop the mask which he was compelled to wear in the presence of all others, and especially in that of the man who, as time went on, seemed more and more to lean on him and find comfort in his companionship.

Vanderlyn had walked the considerable distance from the Avenue du Bois to the quiet street near the Luxembourg where Adèle de Léra lived, and all the way he had felt as if pursued by a mocking demon.

How much longer, so he asked himself, was his awful ordeal to endure? The moments spent by him and Pargeter in Peggy's room had racked heart and memory. He now fled to Madame de Léra as to a refuge from himself.

And yet? Yet he never looked round her pretty sitting-room, with its faded, rather austere furnishings, without being vividly reminded of the woman he had loved and whom he had now lost, for it was there that Peggy had spent the most peaceful hours of her life since Pargeter had first decided that henceforth they should live in Paris.

At last Madame de Léra came into the room; she gave her visitor a quick questioning look. "Have you nothing new to tell?" she asked.

And, after a moment of scarcely perceptible hesitation, Vanderlyn answered, "I have nothing new to tell," but as they both sat down, as he saw how sad and worn the kind face had become in the last three days, there came over him a strong wish to confide in her—to tell her the whole truth. He longed, with morbid longing, to share his knowledge. She, after all, was the only human being who knew the story of his tragic, incomplete love. It would be an infinite comfort and relief to tell her, if not everything, then at least of the irony, the uselessness, of their present search.

Since last night the secret no longer seemed to be his alone.

But Vanderlyn resisted the temptation. He had no right to cast even half his burden on another. Any moment the odious experience which had, it seemed, already befallen Madame de Léra might be repeated. She might again be cross-questioned by the police. In that event it was essential that she should be still able truthfully to declare that she knew nothing.

"I have just come from Tom Pargeter," he observed quietly. "I can't help being sorry for him. The police have been worrying him, and—and at their suggestion we have been seeking among her things—among her correspondence—for some clue. But of course we found nothing. Pargeter is longing to go away—to England. How I wish he would go,—God! how I wish he would go! After all, as he says himself, he can do no good by staying here. He would receive any news within an hour."

Madame de Léra leant forward. "Ah! but if Mr. Pargeter leaves Paris before—before something is discovered, his conduct would be regarded as very cruel—very heartless."

"Did you know," said Vanderlyn, in a low voice, "that Peggy once before disappeared for three days? Pargeter keeps harking back to that. He thinks that she found out something which made her leave him again."

"Yes," said Madame de Léra, "I knew of that episode in their early married life—but on that occasion, Mr. Vanderlyn, our poor friend cannot be said to have disappeared—she only returned to her own family."

"Why, having once escaped, did she ever go back to him?" asked Vanderlyn, sombrely.

"You forget," said Madame de Léra, gently, "that even then there was her son."

Her son? Nay, Vanderlyn at no moment ever forgot Peggy's child. To himself, he seemed to be the only human being who ever thought of the poor little boy lying ill in far-away England.

"Well, you need not be afraid," he said quickly, "that Pargeter will go away to-day. He intends to stay in Paris at least till to-morrow night, for he is convinced, it seems, that the fortune-teller, Madame d'Elphis,—the woman who by some incredible stroke of luck stumbled on the right name of that horse of his which won the Oaks,—will be able to tell him what has happened to—to Margaret Pargeter."

And, meeting Madame de Léra's troubled gaze, he added in a low bitter tone, "How entirely that gives one the measure of the man,—the absurd notion, I mean, that a fortune-teller can solve the mystery! Fortunately or unfortunately, this Madame d'Elphis has been away for two or three days, but she will be back, it seems, in time to give Pargeter, who is a favoured client, an appointment to-morrow morning."

Adèle de Léra suddenly rose from her chair; with a nervous movement she clasped her hands together.

"Ah, but that must not happen!" she exclaimed. "We must think of a way by which we can prevent an interview between Mr. Pargeter and La d'Elphis! Unless," she concluded slowly, "there is no serious reason why he should not know the truth—now?"

Vanderlyn also got up. A look of profound astonishment came over his face.

"The truth?" he repeated. "But surely, Madame de Léra, it is impossible that this woman whom Pargeter is going to consult to-morrow morning can have any clue to the truth! Surely you do not seriously believe——" he did not conclude his sentence. That this broad-minded and religious Frenchwoman could possibly cherish any belief in the type of charlatan to which the American diplomatist supposed the famous Paris fortune-teller to belong was incredible to him.

"I beg of you most earnestly," she repeated, in a deeply troubled voice, "to prevent any meeting between Mr. Pargeter and Madame d'Elphis! Believe me, I do not speak without reason; I know more of this soothsayer and her mysterious powers than you can possibly know——"

"Do you mean me to understand that you yourself would ever consult such an oracle?" Vanderlyn could not keep a certain contemptuous incredulity out of his voice.

"No, indeed! But then I, unlike you, believe this woman's traffic to be of the devil. Listen, Mr. Vanderlyn, and I will tell you of a case in which La d'Elphis was closely concerned—a case of which I have absolute knowledge."

Madame de Léra went back to her chair; she sank into it, and, with Vanderlyn standing before her, she told him the story.

"If you cast back your mind to the time when you were first in Paris, you will probably recall my husband's niece, a beautiful girl named Jeanne de Léra?" Vanderlyn bent his head without speaking; nay more, a look of pain came over his tired face, and sunken eyes, for, strangely enough, there was a certain sinister parallel between the fate which had befallen the charming girl whose image was thus suddenly brought up before him, and that of the beloved woman who seemed to be now even more present to his emotional memory than she had been in life.

"As you know, for it was no secret, Jeanne had what English and American people call 'flirted' with Henri Delavigne, and he had sworn that he would kill himself on her wedding-day. Well, the poor foolish girl took this threat very seriously; it shadowed her happy betrothal, and on the very day before her marriage was to take place, she persuaded her married sister to go with her to a fortune-teller. It was not her own future, which stretched cloudless and radiant before her, that tempted Jeanne to peer into these mysteries; she only wished to be reassured as to Delavigne and his absurd threat———"

Madame de Léra stopped speaking a moment, and then she went on—

"Madame d'Elphis had just then become the rage, and so Jeanne decided to consult her, although the woman charged a higher fee than, I understand, the other fortune-tellers were then doing. When the two sisters found themselves there, my married niece bargained that the séance should be half-price, as Jeanne only wished to stay a very few minutes, and to ask but one question. After the bargain was concluded, Jeanne, it seems, observed—the story of the interview has been told to me, and before me, many many times—that she hoped the fortune-teller would take as much trouble as if she had paid the full fee. On this the woman replied, with a rather malignant smile, 'I can assure Mademoiselle that she will have plenty for her money!'

"Then began the séance. La d'Elphis gave, as those sorts of people always do, a marvellously accurate account of the poor child's past,—the simple, virginal past of a very young girl,—but when it came to the future, she declared that her vision had become blurred, and that she could see nothing! Nothing! Nothing! Both the sisters pressed her to say more, to predict something of the future; and at last, speaking very reluctantly, she admitted that she saw Jeanne, pale, deathly pale, clad in a wedding-dress, and she also evoked a wonderful vision of white flowers...."

Madame de Léra looked up at her visitor, but Vanderlyn made no comment; and so she went on:—

"Then, with some confusion, Jeanne summoned up courage to ask the one question she had come there to ask. The answer came at once, and was more than reassuring: 'As to the man concerning whom you are so anxious,' said Madame d'Elphis, 'you may count on his fidelity. The years will go on and others who loved you will forget you—but he will ever remember.' 'Then nothing will happen to him to-morrow?' asked Jeanne eagerly. 'To-morrow?' replied the woman, mysteriously, 'To-morrow I see him plunged in deep grief, and yet that which has brought him this awful sorrow will not perhaps be wholly regretted by him.'

"My poor little niece, if rather piqued, was yet much relieved, and the two sisters left the presence of this horrible, sinister creature."

Madame de Léra passed her hand with a nervous movement over her mouth—"It was while they were actually driving home from this séance with La d'Elphis that the terrible accident, which you of course remember, occurred,—an accident which resulted in the younger sister's death, while the elder miraculously escaped unhurt. Jeanne was buried in her wedding-dress—and the flowers—you recall the wonderful flowers? The woman's predictions as to Delavigne's constancy came strangely true; who now remembers Jeanne, save her poor mother—and Delavigne?"

"Yes, it's a very curious, striking story," said Vanderlyn, slowly, "but—forgive me for saying so—if your niece's marriage had taken place on the morrow, would anything of all this have been remembered by either herself or her sister? The predictions of Madame d'Elphis were of a kind which it would be safe to make of any French girl, belonging to your world, on the eve of her marriage——"

He stopped abruptly. In his wearied and yet morbidly active mind, an idea, a suggestion, of which he was half-ashamed, was beginning to germinate.

"I should be grateful," he said, slowly, "if you can tell me something more about La d'Elphis. I am quite sure that I shall not be able to prevent an interview between her and Pargeter,—but still something might be done— Is she respectable? Can she, for example,"—his eyes dropped,—"be bribed?"

Madame de Léra looked at Vanderlyn keenly. Perhaps she saw farther into his mind than an American or an Englishwoman would have done.

"All these sorts of people can be bribed," she said, quietly. "As to her private life, I know nothing of it, but either of my nephews would be able to tell you whatever is known of her, for since that tragic affair our family have always taken a morbid interest in La d'Elphis. Would you like to know something about her now, at once? Shall I send for my nephew?"

In answer to Vanderlyn's look, rather than to his muttered assent, Madame de Léra left the room.

During the few moments of her absence, a plan began to elaborate itself with insistent clearness in Vanderlyn's mind; he saw, or thought he saw, that here might be an issue out of his terrible dilemma. And yet, even while so seeing the way become clear before him, he felt a deep, instinctive repugnance from the method which would have to be employed....

There came the sound of footsteps, and, turning his back to the window, he prepared himself for the inevitable question with which, during the last three days, almost everyone he met had greeted him.

But the youth who came into the room with Madame de Léra, if a typical Parisian in the matter of his careful, rather foppish, dress, and in his bored expression, yet showed that he was possessed of the old-fashioned good breeding which is still to be found in France, if only in that peculiar section of French society known collectively as "the faubourg." Jacques de Léra, alone among the many men whom Vanderlyn had come across since the disappearance of Mrs. Pargeter had become the talk of the town, made no allusion to the mystery, and asked no puerile question of the man who was known to be her friend.

"Mr. Vanderlyn has been asking me what I knew of the fortune-teller, Madame d'Elphis. But, beyond the story concerning your poor cousin Jeanne, I know nothing. You, Jacques, will doubtless be able to tell us something of her. Is it true, for instance, that she is sometimes employed by the police? I seem to have heard so—not lately, but long ago?"

"They say so," said Jacques de Léra, casting a quick glance at Vanderlyn. "They say she helped to catch Pranzini. Extraordinary stories are told of her gifts. But none of us have ever been at all anxious to consult her—after poor Jeanne's affair. You may have seen her,"—he turned to Vanderlyn,—"for she's sometimes at first nights and at private views. She's by way of being artistic and cultivated; and though she's strikingly handsome, she dresses oddly—poses as a Muse."

"She must make a great deal of money," said Madame de Léra, thoughtfully; with a half smile she asked her nephew the question: "Is there a Monsieur d'Elphis? Are there infant oracles?"

Jacques burst out laughing, and both Vanderlyn and Madame de Léra started. It was the first time for many days that they had heard the sound of simple human laughter.

"My dear aunt," said the young man, chuckling, "the husband—*qua* husband—is, I assure you, an unknown animal in that strange underworld of which our beautiful city is the chosen Mecca. No, no, Madame d'Elphis does not waste her time in producing little oracles! If you wish to hear the truth, I mean the whole truth, I will tell it you."

And then, as Madame de Léra nodded her head, he added, more seriously, "La d'Elphis is one of two sisters, the daughters of a very respectable notary at Orange. Both threw their caps over the windmill, the one to become an unsuccessful actress, the other a successful soothsayer. La d'Elphis has one virtue—she is a devoted sister, and lives with the other's *smalah*. As to her own private life, she has been for many years the friend of Achille de Florac. She became acquainted with him not long before his final crash; who knows, perhaps she helped to precipitate it! It is to be hoped she did, for since then he has practically lived on her. And so, my dear aunt, she is in a sense our cousin *de la main gauche*!"

Vanderlyn looked away from Madame de Léra. He was sorry the young man had been so frank, for the Marquis de Florac was not only by birth a member of her circle, but he was, as Jacques rather cruelly pointed out, a connection of the de Léra family.

"Poor creature!" exclaimed Adèle de Léra; her voice was filled with involuntary pity.

"Yes," continued Jacques, in answer to her look, "you may well say 'poor creature!' For it's from La d'Elphis that our disreputable cousin draws the major part of his uncertain revenues. When Paris is credulous, his credit goes up, and he has plenty of money to play with. I'm told that the other night he lost ten thousand francs at 'Monaco Junior'!"

Vanderlyn made a slight movement. "Yes," he said, "that is true,—I was there."

"In the lean months," continued Jacques, who did not often find his conversation listened to with such respect and attention as was now the case, "I mean, of course, in the summer—poor Florac has to retrench, but La d'Elphis does not remain idle. She goes to Aix, to Vichy, to Dieppe for the Grande Semaine,—in fact, wherever rich foreigners gather; and wherever she goes she finds plenty eager to consult her!"

"Is that all you wanted to know?" said Madame de Léra to Vanderlyn.

"Yes," he said, slowly, "that is all. I did not know—I had no idea—that our poor old world was still so credulous!"

XI.

As Vanderlyn walked away from Madame de Léra's door, the plan, of which the first outline had come to him while she was telling the strange story concerning the fortune-teller and her niece, had taken final shape; and it now impressed itself upon him as the only way out of his terrible dilemma.

Vanderlyn was by nature a truthful man, and in spite of the ambiguous nature of his relations with Margaret Pargeter, he had never been compelled to lie in defence of their friendship. Even during these last few days, he had as far as was possible avoided untruth, and only to one person, that is, to the Prefect of Police, had he lied—lied desperately, and lied successfully. This was why, even while telling himself that he had at last found a way in which to convey the truth to Pargeter, he felt a deep repugnance from the methods which he saw he would be compelled to employ.

More than once the American diplomatist had had occasion to take part in delicate negotiations with one of those nameless, countryless individuals, whose ideal it is to be in the pay of a foreign Embassy, and who always set on their ignoble services a far higher value than those services generally deserve. But Vanderlyn belonged to the type of man who finds it far easier to fight for others, and especially for his country, than for himself. Still, in this case, was he not fighting for Margaret Pargeter? For what he knew she valued far more than life itself—her honour. What he was about to do was hateful to him—he was aware how severely he would have judged such conduct in another—but it seemed the only way, a way made miraculously possible by the superstitious folly of Tom Pargeter.

The offer Vanderlyn was about to convey to Madame d'Elphis was quite simple; in exchange for saying a very few words to Tom Pargeter,—words which would add greatly to the belief the millionaire already possessed in what he took to be her extraordinary gifts of divination,—the soothsayer would receive ten thousand francs.

There need be no difficulty even as to the words she should use to reveal the truth; Vanderlyn had cut out from the *Petit Journal* the paragraph which told of the strange discovery made three nights before at Orange. He would inform her that Mr. Pargeter's friends, having assured themselves that the unknown woman in question was Mrs. Pargeter, desired to break the sad news through her, instead of in a more commonplace fashion.

Vanderlyn knew enough of that curious underworld of Paris which preys on wealthy foreigners, to feel sure that this would not be the first time that Madame d'Elphis had been persuaded, in her own interest, to add the agreeable ingredient of certainty to one of her predictions. The diplomatist also believed he could carry through the negotiation without either revealing his identity, or giving the soothsayer any clue to his reason for making her so strange a proposal.

Having made his plan, Vanderlyn found it remarkably easy to carry out.

In London, such a man as himself would have found it difficult to have ascertained at a moment's notice the address of even a famous palmist or fortune-teller. But in everything to do with social life Paris is highly organised, London singularly chaotic.

On reaching home, he at once discovered, with a certain bitter amusement, that Madame d'Elphis disdained the artifices with which she might reasonably have surrounded her mysterious craft. Not only were her name, address, and even hours of consultation, to be found in the "Tout Paris," but there also was inscribed her telephone number.

Vanderlyn hated the telephone. He never used it unless he was compelled to do so; but now he went through the weary, odious preliminaries with a certain eagerness—"Alo! Alo! Alo!"

At last a woman's voice answered, "Yes—yes. Who is it?"

"Can Madame d'Elphis receive a client this evening?"

There was a pause. Then he heard a question asked, a murmured answer of which the sense evaded him, and then a refusal,—not, he fancied, a very decided refusal,—followed by a discreet attempt to discover his name, his nationality, his address, with a suggestion that Madame d'Elphis would be at his disposal the next morning.

A touch of doubt in the quick, hesitating accents of the unseen woman emboldened Vanderlyn. He conveyed, civilly and clearly, that he was quite prepared to offer a very special fee for the favour he was asking; and he indicated that, though he had been told the usual price of a séance was fifty francs, he—the mysterious stranger who was speaking to Madame d'Elphis through the telephone—was so exceedingly anxious to be received by her that evening that he would pay a fancy fee,—in fact as much as a thousand francs,—for the privilege of consulting the famous fortune-teller.

To Vanderlyn's vexation and surprise, there followed a long pause.

At last came the answer, the expected assent; but it was couched in words which surprised and vaguely disquieted him.

"Very well, sir, my sister will be ready to receive you at eight o'clock to-night; but she is going out, so she will not be able to give you a prolonged séance."

Then he had not been speaking to the soothsayer herself? Vanderlyn felt vaguely disquieted and discomfited. He had counted on having to take but one person into his half-confidence; and then—well, he had told himself while at the telephone that he would not find it difficult to conclude the bargain he desired to make with the woman whose highly-pitched, affected voice had given him, or so he had thought, the clue to a venal personality.

It was with a feeling of considerable excitement and curiosity that the diplomatist, that same evening, walked up the quiet, now deserted, streets where dwelt the most famous of Parisian fortune-tellers.

Madame d'Elphis had chosen a prosaic setting for the scene of her mysteries, for the large white house looked very new, a huge wedge of modern ugliness in the pretty old street, its ugliness made the more apparent by its proximity to one of those leafy gardens which form oases of fragrant stillness in the more ancient quarters of the town.

A curt answer was given by the concierge in reply to Vanderlyn's enquiry for Madame d'Elphis. "Walk through the courtyard; the person you seek occupies the entresol of the house you will see there."

And then he saw that lying back, quite concealed from the street, was another and very different type of dwelling, and one far more suited to the requirements of even a latter-day soothsayer.

As he made his way over the dimly-lighted, ill-paved court which separated the new building, that giving onto the street, from the seventeenth-century mansion, Vanderlyn realised that his first impression had been quite erroneous. Madame d'Elphis had evidently gauged, and that very closely, the effect she desired to produce on her patrons. Even in the daytime the mansarded house which now gloomed before him must look secret, mysterious. Behind such narrow latticed windows might well have dwelt Cagliostro, or, further back, the more sinister figure of La Voison.

But something of this feeling left him as he passed through the door which gave access to the old house; and, as he began to walk up the shabby gas-lit staircase, he felt that his repugnant task would be an easy one. The woman who, living here, allowed herself the luxury of such a lover as was the Marquis de Florac, would not—nay, could not—hesitate before such an offer as ten thousand francs.

There was but one door on the entresol, and on its panel was inscribed in small gold letters the word "d'Elphis." As Vanderlyn rang the bell, the odd name gleamed at him in the gas-light.

There followed a considerable delay, but at last he saw a face peering at him through the little grating—significantly styled a *Judas*, and doubtless dating from the Revolution,—still to be found in many an old-fashioned Parisian front-door.

The inspection having apparently proved satisfactory, the door opened, and Vanderlyn was admitted, by a young *bonne à tout faire*, into a hall filled with a strong smell of cooking, a smell that made it clear that Madame d'Elphis and her family—her *smalah*, as Jacques de Léra had called them—had the true Southern love of garlic.

Without asking his name or business, the servant showed him straight into a square, gold-and-white salon. Standing there, forgetful for a moment of his distasteful errand, Vanderlyn looked about him with mingled contempt and disgust, for his eyes, trained to observe, had at once become aware that the note of this room was showy vulgarity. The furniture was a mixture of imitation Louis XV. and sham Empire. On the woven tapestry sofa lay a child's toy, once costly, but now broken.

How amazing the fact that here, amid these pretentiously ugly and commonplace surroundings, innumerable human beings had stood, and would stand, trembling with fear, suspense, and hope! Vanderlyn reminded himself that here also Tom Pargeter, a man accustomed to measure everything by the money standard, had waited many a time in the sure belief that this was the ante-chamber to august and awe-inspiring mysteries; here, all unknowing of what the future held, he would come to-morrow morning, to learn, for once, the truth—the terrible truth—from the charlatan to whom he, poor fool, pinned his faith.

Suddenly a door opened, and Vanderlyn turned round with eager curiosity, a curiosity which became merged in astonishment. The woman advancing towards him made her vulgar surroundings sink into blurred insignificance; for Madame d'Elphis, with her slight, sinuous figure, draped in a red peplum, her pale face lit by dark tragic eyes, looked the sybil to the life....

Vanderlyn bowed, with voluntary deference. "Monsieur," she said, in a low, deep voice, "I must ask you to follow me; this is my sister's *appartement*. I live next door."

She preceding him, they walked through an untidy dining-room of which the furniture—the sham Renaissance chairs and walnut-wood buffet—looked strangely alien to Vanderlyn's guide, into a short, ill-lighted passage, which terminated in a locked, handleless door.

The woman whom he now knew to be Madame d'Elphis turned, and, facing Vanderlyn, for the first time allowed her melancholy eyes to rest full on her unknown visitor.

"You have your stick, your hat?" she asked. "Yes?—that is well; for when our séance is over, you will leave by another way, a way which leads into the garden, and so into the street."

She unlocked the door, and he followed her into a large book-lined study—masculine in its sober colouring and simple furnishings. Above the mantelpiece was arranged a trophy of swords and fencing-sticks; opposite hung a superb painting by Henner. Vanderlyn remembered having seen this picture exhibited in the Salon some five years before. It had been shown under the title "The Crystal-Gazer," and it was even now an admirable portrait of his hostess, for so, unconsciously, had Vanderlyn begun to regard the woman who was so little like what he had expected to find her.

Madame d'Elphis beckoned to him to follow her into yet another, and a much smaller, room. Ah! This was evidently the place where she pursued her strange calling; for here—so Vanderlyn, trying to combat the eerie impression she produced on him, sardonically told himself—were the stage properties of her singular craft.

The high walls were hung with red cloth, against which gleamed innumerable plaster casts of hands. The only furniture consisted of a round, polished table, which took up a good deal of the space in the room; on the table stood an old-fashioned lamp, and in the middle of the circle of light cast by the lamp on its shining surface, a round crystal ball. Two chairs were drawn up to the table.

An extraordinary sensation of awe—of vague disquiet—crept over Laurence Vanderlyn; he suddenly remembered the tragic story of Jeanne de Léra. Was it here that the sinister interview with the doomed girl had taken place?

It was Madame d'Elphis who broke the long silence:—

"I must ask you, Monsieur," she said, stiffly, "to depose the fee on the table. It is the custom."

Vanderlyn's thin nervous hand shot up to his mouth to hide a smile; the eerie feeling which had so curiously possessed him dropped away, leaving him slightly ashamed.

"Poor woman," he said to himself, "she cannot even divine that I am an honest man!"

He bent his head gravely, and took the roll of notes with which he had come provided out of his pocket. He placed a thousand-franc note on the table. "What a fool she must think me!" he mentally exclaimed; then came the consoling reflection, "But she won't think me a fool for long."

Madame d'Elphis scarcely glanced at the thousand-franc note; she left it lying where Vanderlyn had put it. "Will you please sit down, Monsieur?" she said.

Vanderlyn rather reluctantly obeyed her. As she seated herself opposite to him, he was struck by the sad intensity of her face; he told himself that she had once been—nay, that she was still—beautiful, but it was the tortured beauty of a woman who lives by and through her emotions.

He also realised that his task would not be quite as easy as he had hoped it would be; the manner of La d'Elphis was cold, correct, and ladylike—no other word would serve—to the point of severity. He saw that he would have to word his offer of a bribe in as least offensive a fashion as was possible. But while he was trying to find a sentence with which to embark on the delicate negotiation, he suddenly felt his left hand grasped and turned over, with a firm and yet impersonal touch.

The centre of the soothsayer's cool palm rested itself on the ring—his mother's wedding ring—loosely encircling his little finger, and then Madame d'Elphis began speaking in a low, quiet, and yet hesitating, voice,—a voice which suddenly recalled to her listener her Southern birth and breeding; it was strangely unlike the accents in which she had asked him to produce the promised fee.

Surprise, a growing, ever-deepening surprise, kept Vanderlyn silent. He soon forgot completely, for the time being, the business which had brought him there.

"For you the crystal," she whispered, "for others the Grand Jeu. You have not come, as others do, to learn the future; you do not care what happens to you—now."

She waited a moment, then, "the ring brings with it two visions," she said, fixing her eyes on the polished depths before her. "Visions of love and death—of pain and parting; one, if clear, yet recedes far into the past...."

She raised her voice, and began speaking in a monotonous recitative:

"I see you with a woman standing in a garden; behind you both is a great expanse of water. She is so like you that I think she must be your mother. She wears her grey hair in Madonna bands; she puts her arms round your neck; as she does so, I see on her left hand one ring—the ring which you are now wearing, and which I am now touching. She, your mother, is bidding you good-bye, she knows that she will never see you again, but you do not know it, so she smiles, for she is a brave woman——"

Madame d'Elphis stopped speaking. Vanderlyn stared at her with a sense of growing excitement and amazement; he was telling himself that this woman undoubtedly possessed the power of reading not only the minds, but even the emotional memories, of those who came to consult her.... Yes, it was true; his last parting with his mother had been out of doors, in the garden of their own family house on the shores of Lake Champlain.

As he looked fixedly at the crystal-gazer's downcast eyes, his own emotions seemed to become reflected in her countenance. She grasped his hand with a firmer, a more convulsive pressure.

"I see you again," she exclaimed, "and again with a woman! This vision is very clear; it evokes the immediate past—almost the present. The woman is young; her hair is fair, and in a cloud about her head. You are together on a journey. It is night——"

Madame d'Elphis stopped speaking abruptly; she looked up at Vanderlyn, and he saw that her dark eyes were brimming with tears, her mouth quivering.

"Do you wish me to describe what I see?" she asked, in an almost inaudible voice.

"No," said Vanderlyn, hoarsely,—he seemed to feel Peggy's arms about his neck, her soft lips brushing his cheek.

The soothsayer bent down till her face was within a few inches of the polished surface into which she was gazing.

"Now she is lying down," she whispered. "Her face is turned away. Is she asleep? No, she is dead!—dead!"

"Can you see her now?" asked Vanderlyn. "For God's sake tell me where she is! Can I hope to see her again—once more?"

Madame d'Elphis withdrew her hand from that of Vanderlyn.

"You will only see her face," she answered, slowly, "through the coffin-lid. That you will see. As to where she is now—I see her clearly, and yet,"—she went on, as if to herself, "nay, but that's impossible! I see her," she went on, raising her voice, "laid out for burial under a shed in a beautiful garden. The garden is that of Dr. Fortoul's house at Orange. At the head of the pallet on which she lies there are two blessed candles; a nun kneels on the ground. Stay,—who is that coming in from the garden? It is the wife of the doctor, it is Madame Fortoul,"—again there came a note of wavering doubt into the voice of the crystal-gazer. "She is whispering to the nun, and I hear her words; she says, 'Poor child, she is young, too young to have died like this, alone. I am having a mass said for her soul to-morrow morning.'"

Madame d'Elphis looked up. Her large eyes, of which the lids were slightly reddened, rested on Vanderlyn's pale, drawn face.

"Monsieur," she said, in a low, reluctant voice, "to be honest with you, I fear I have been leading you astray. During the last few moments it is my own past life that has been rising before me, not the present of this poor dead woman. When I am tired—and I am very tired to-night—some such trick is sometimes played me. I was born at Orange; as a child I spent many hours in the beautiful garden which just now rose up before me; I once saw a dead body in that shed—Madame Fortoul, who is devout, often has masses said for those who meet with sudden deaths and whose bodies are brought to her husband."

The soothsayer rose from her chair.

"If you will come to me to-morrow," she said, "bringing with you something which belonged to this lady, I am sure I shall be able to tell you all you wish to know. For that second séance," she added hurriedly, "I shall of course ask no further fee."

Vanderlyn, waking as from a dream, heard sounds in the other room, the coming and going of a man's footsteps. He also got up.

"Madame," he said, quietly, "I thank you from my heart. I recognise the truth of all you have told me, *with one paramount exception*. It is true that the woman whom you saw lying dead is now in the house of Dr. Fortoul at Orange; the fact that you once knew the place is an accident—and nothing but an accident. You have, however, Madame, made one strange mistake."

He took out of his pocket and held in his hand the large open envelope containing, in addition to the remainder of the notes he had brought, the slip he had cut from the newspaper. "Here is the proof that all you have seen is true," he repeated, "with one exception—*This lady was alone in the train*. It is important that this should be thoroughly understood by you, for to-morrow you will be called upon to testify to the fact."

Madame d'Elphis stiffened into deep attention.

"To-morrow morning," continued Vanderlyn, very deliberately, "one of your regular clients is coming to ask you to assist him to solve a terrible mystery. I will tell you his name—it is Mr. Pargeter, the well-known sportsman. He is coming to ask you to help him to find Mrs. Pargeter, who some days ago mysteriously disappeared. This lady's death, but he does not yet know it, took place while she was travelling—travelling alone. I repeat, Madame, that she was *alone—quite alone—on her fatal journey*."

Vanderlyn stopped speaking a moment; then his voice lowered, became troubled and beseeching.

"Once you have revealed the truth to Mr. Pargeter,—and he will believe implicitly all you say,—then, Madame, you will not only have accomplished a good action, but a sum, bringing the fee for the séance which is just concluded up to ten thousand francs, will be placed at your disposal by me."

Madame d'Elphis looked long and searchingly at the man standing before her.

"Monsieur," she said, "will you give me your word that the death of Mrs. Pargeter was as this paper declares it to have been—that is to say, a natural death?"

"Yes," answered Vanderlyn, "she knew that she would die in this way—suddenly."

"Then," said the fortune-teller, coldly, "I will do as you desire."

Vanderlyn, following a sudden impulse, put the envelope he held in his hand on the table. "Here is the fee," he said, briefly. "I know that I can trust in your discretion, your loyalty,—may I add, Madame, in your kindness?"

"I am ashamed," she whispered, "ashamed to take this money." She clasped her hands together in an unconscious gesture of supplication, and then asked, with a curious childish directness, "It is a great deal—can you afford it, Monsieur?"

"Yes," he said, hastily; the suffering, shamed expression on her face moved him strangely.

"When you next see Mr. Pargeter," she murmured, "you shall have written proof that I have carried out your wish."

She tapped the table twice, sharply,—then led the way into the larger room. It was empty, but Vanderlyn, even as he entered, saw a door closing quietly.

Madame d'Elphis walked across to an un-curtained window; she opened it and stepped through on to a broad terrace balcony.

"Walk down the iron stairway," she said, in a low voice, "there are not many steps. A little door leads from the garden below straight into the street; the door has been left unlocked to-night."

Vanderlyn held out his hand; she took it and held it for a moment. "Ah!" she said, softly, "would that *I* had died when I was still young, still beautiful, still loved!—"

XII.

The bright May sun was pouring into Tom Pargeter's large smoking-room, making more alive and vivid the fantastic and brilliantly-coloured posters lining the walls.

Laurence Vanderlyn, standing there in a peopled solitude, caught a glimpse of his own strained and tired face in a mirror which filled up the space between two windows, and what he saw startled him, for it seemed to him that none could look at his countenance and not see written there the tale of his anguish, remorse, and suspense. And yet he knew that now his ordeal was drawing to a close; in a few moments Pargeter was due to return from his interview with Madame d'Elphis.

Walking up and down the sunny room which held for him such agonising memories of the long hours spent there during the last three days in Tom Pargeter's company, Vanderlyn lived again every moment of his own strange interview with the soothsayer. The impression of sincerity which Madame d'Elphis had produced on him had now had time to fade, and he asked himself with nervous dread whether she was, after all, likely to do what she had promised. Nay, was it in her power to lie,—or rather to tell the half-truth which was all that he had asked her to tell?

At last there came the sound of the front-door of the villa opening, shutting; and then those made by Pargeter's quick, short footsteps striking the marble floor of the hall, and echoing through the silent house.

Vanderlyn stopped short in his restless pacing. He turned and waited.

The door was flung open, and Pargeter came in. Quietly shutting the door behind him, he walked down the room to where the other man, with his back to the window, stood waiting for him. The three days and nights which had carved indelible lines on the American's already seamed face, had left Pargeter's untouched; just now he looked grave, subdued, but his face had lost the expression of perplexed anger and anxiety which had alone betrayed the varying emotions he had experienced since the disappearance of his wife.

At last, when close to Vanderlyn, he spoke—in a low, gruff whisper. "Grid!" he exclaimed, "Grid, old man, don't be shocked! La d'Elphis says that Peggy's dead—that she's been dead three days!"

Vanderlyn could not speak. He stared dumbly at the other, and as he realised the relief, almost the joy, in Pargeter's voice, there came over him a horrible impulse to strike—and then to flee.

"There, you can see it for yourself—" Pargeter held out, with fingers twitching with excitement, a sheet of note-paper. "La d'Elphis wrote it all down! I didn't see her—she's ill. But this is not the first time I've had to work her in that way, and it does just as well. Her sister managed everything,—she took her in one of Peggy's gloves which I'd brought with me."

Vanderlyn shuddered. He opened his mouth, but no words would come. Then he looked down at the sheet of paper Pargeter had handed him:—

"The person to whom this glove belonged has been dead three days. She died on a journey—alone. Think of the bridal flower,—it will guide you to where she now lies waiting for those who loved her to claim her."

Pargeter laid one hand on Vanderlyn's arm—with the other he took out of one of his pockets a sheaf of thin slips of paper. The American knew them to contain accounts of accidents and untoward occurrences registered at the Prefecture of Police.

Pargeter detached one of the slips and laid it across the sheet of paper on which Madame d'Elphis had written her laconic message:—

"Look—look at *this*, Grid! And don't say again I'm a fool for believing in La d'Elphis! I've had this since the day before yesterday; but I didn't bother to show it to you, for I didn't think anything of it—I shouldn't now, but for La d'Elphis! But do look—'the body of a young, fair woman found in a train at *Orange*,'—'the bridal flower,' as La d'Elphis says—eh, what?"

But still Vanderlyn did not speak.

"I've thought it all out," Pargeter went on, excitedly. "Peggy was driven to the wrong station—see? Got into the wrong train—and then—then, Grid, when she found out what she'd done, she got upset——" For the first time a note of awe, of horror, came into his voice—"You see, my sister Sophy was right, after all; the poor girl's heart was queer!"

"And what are you going to do now?" asked Vanderlyn in a low, dry tone. "Arrange for a special to Orange, I suppose? What time will you start, Tom? Would you like me to come with you?"

Pargeter reddened; his green eye blinked as if he felt suddenly blinded by the bright sun.

"I'm not thinking of going myself," he said, rather ashamedly. "Where would be the good of it? Her brother and that cousin of hers are sure to want to go. They can take Plimmer. The truth is—well, old man, I don't feel up to it! I've always had an awful horror of death. Peggy knew that well enough——" the colour faded from his face; he looked at the other with a nervous, dejected expression.

"Tom," said Vanderlyn, slowly, "why shouldn't *I* go to Orange—with Madame de Léra? Why say anything to Peggy's people till we really know?"

For the first time Pargeter seemed moved to genuine human feeling. "Well," he said, "you *are* a good friend, Grid! I'll never forget how you've stood by me during this worrying time. I wish I could do something for you in return——" he looked at the other doubtfully. To poor Tom Pargeter, "doing something" always meant parting with money, and Laurence Vanderlyn was, if not rich, then quite well off.

Vanderlyn's hand suddenly shook. He dropped the piece of paper he had been holding. "Perhaps you'll let me have Jasper sometimes—in the holidays," he said, huskily.

"Lord, yes! Of course I will! There's nothing would please poor Peggy more! Then—then when will you start, Grid? I mean for Orange?"

"At once," said Vanderlyn. Then he looked long, hesitatingly at Pargeter, and the millionaire, with most unusual perspicacity, read and answered the question contained in that strange, uncertain gaze.

"Don't bring her back, Grid! I couldn't stand a big funeral here. I don't want to hear any more about it than I can help! Of course, it isn't much good my going over to England *now*, but I won't stay in Paris, I'll get away,—right away for a bit, on the yacht,—and take some of the crowd with me."

No one ever knew the truth. To the Prefect of Police the mystery of the disappearance of Mrs. Pargeter is still unsolved—unsolvable. When he meets a pretty woman out at dinner he tells her the story—and asks her what she thinks.

As for Laurence Vanderlyn, he has gone home—home to the old colonial house which was built by his great-grandfather, the friend of Franklin, on the shores of Lake Champlain. He never speaks of Peggy excepting to Jasper; but to the lad he sometimes talks of her as if she were still there, still very near to them both, near enough to be grieved if her boy should ever forget that he had a mother who loved him dearly.

THE END.

Milton Keynes UK
Ingram Content Group UK Ltd.
UKHW030742071024
449371UK00006B/617

9 789362 093646